FRANCE

CW01597142

FRANCE AT A GLANCE

(A holiday handbook for all)

INGE and JAMES MOORE

SETTLE and BENDALL (WIGMORE)

© 1984 Inge and James Moore
All rights reserved. No part of this publication
may be reproduced or transmitted in any form or
by any means without permission.
First published in 1984 by Settle and Bendall (Wigmore)
32 Savile Row
London W1X 1AG
ISBN (Hardback) 0 907070 15 9
(Paperback) 0 907070 16 7

Printed by Villiers Publications Ltd
Ingestre Road, London NW5 1UL

CONTENTS

ACKNOWLEDGEMENT

We would especially like to thank Mrs Pauline Hallam and her staff at the F.G.T.O. in London for their very willing and cheerful help throughout our work on the book.

INTRODUCTION

France at a Glance is a guide for anyone who goes to France, no matter from which country they come, no matter what purpose their visit has. Above all it is meant to help people to feel at home as quickly as possible, to avoid the usual pitfalls which beset them and to cope with the very French way in which things are done.

The information is based on the authors' personal experiences over many years of travel in France. This is a country where the inhabitants place much store by the effort foreigners make to understand their customs and by their appreciation of its beauty and rich and varied cuisine.

It is essentially a handbook covering just about every aspect of everday life as it concerns the visitor. How to shop, how to use the telephone, what kind of accommodation to seek, what to expect in restaurants and what culinary specialities to savour are all included. Much information is given on the subject of motoring, the transport method that most people use to journey around this very large country. The French make good use of their extensive network of mainly good roads and this guide provides many helpful hints on route planning.

Equipped with the information we have accumulated over the years, we hope and believe that you will derive more enjoyment and better value from your visit to one of the most varied and exciting countries in Europe.

Bon Voyage!

ADVANCE INFORMATION*

French Government Tourist Offices

The French Government operates a public information service in many countries. The French Government Tourist Office in London publishes annually a short Holiday Reference Guide that answers most questions asked by most people most of the time and gives addresses of villa companies, tour operators, caravan operators, package tour operators and hotel groups. This and other printed information material specifically asked for (e.g. brochures on regions, towns, hotel lists, list of events) can be obtained by writing to the F.G.T.O. and enclosing 5 × 10p stamps. Urgent telephone enquiries can be made between 9 a.m. and 5 p.m. Monday to Friday, but lines tend to get extremely busy. For personal callers, who are welcome, there is a mass of printed information to take away and a photo-file of hotels and camp sites to be consulted. The F.G.T.O. does not make bookings!

In France

Regional
For more detailed advance information about the French regions you can write to the Regional Tourist Committees, of which there are 24, including Paris. These offices do not answer telephone enquiries and cannot deal with personal callers. They do not make bookings. Enquiries can be made in English.

Departmental
A relatively new institution is the *Loisirs-Accueil* Reservation Service (*Loisir-Accueil* meaning, literally, 'leisure welcome'). The object of these non-profit-making booking offices, which

---

*A complete list of addresses for this and following chapters can be found on pp.185-192.

will eventually be set up in most *départements*, is to offer a centralised booking service, covering the whole *département*, for hotels, *gîtes ruraux* (see p.38), *chambres d'hôtes* (bed and breakfast on the farm), camp sites and special interest holidays (sports activities, pony-trekking, holidays afloat, archaeology, cookery and art courses etc.). *Loisirs-Accueil* booking offices are open all the year round and will handle advance bookings following enquiries in writing or by telephone from the UK. Most of them have English-speaking staff so that communications should be no problem. For special interest holidays you should first write or telephone for a brochure. Unfortunately, these cannot be booked in July or August. Anything booked through a *Loisirs-Accueil* office has to be paid for in advante: 25% on acceptance of the booking and the balance 30 days prior to departure.

Locally

Most towns in France, even the smaller ones and especially those in favoured tourist regions, have a tourist information office, which is signposted either as *Office de Tourisme* or *Syndicat d'Initiative*. Often the sign directing you to it in a town will simply depict the letter 'i' in a square. Addresses and closing days are listed under the local entries in the red Michelin guide.

The *Office de Tourisme/Syndicat d'Initiative* is the place to go if you want any local information whatsoever, not only lists of hotels, restaurants, local events and sights but advice on opening hours, or where to find the nearest *hypermarché* or swimming pool. The local *Syndicat d'Initiative* is the first place to go when you arrive in a place where you intend to spend some time. Most *Syndicats* do not make hotel bookings, though, except those with a specific booking service called *Accueil de France* (nothing to do with Loisirs-Accueil, see above). There are about 35 of these in large towns all over France; a list can be obtained from the F.G.T.O. in London. They make bookings for personal callers only and solely for a maximum of 7 days in advance, including the same day.

Parlez-Vous Français?

The question of how well one can hope to get by in France without a knowledge of French is frequently aimed at the French National Tourist Office by would-be travellers who are cautious of venturing into what is, by general consent, a rather chauvinistic nation of decidedly unenthusiastic linguists. Whether you should put yourself out to speak their language depends on what you want to do or expect to get out of a holiday in France. There is no doubt that if you are staying in a village and want to mingle with the French in their everyday lives, to chat with the butcher, the baker and the grocer, then you really need a fair smattering of French. With a bit of practice you can get by with schoolboy French of O-level standard, so long as you have a dictionary or phrasebook to hand. If you try hard you will find a sympathetic ear and you will enjoy your holiday all the more for having made a real contact.

If you are simply intent on making straight for the sun and plan to remain among your compatriots for the bulk of the holiday, then a knowledge of French, apart from a few basic words, is rather superfluous. If pushed, a fair number of Frenchmen can cope with basic English, much as we cope with basic French.

2. MAPS, GUIDES AND FINDING YOUR WAY ABOUT

Assuming that one is restricted to choosing just one range of maps and guides, there can be no question that top of the list are the Michelin publications. For many years this famous tyre company has dominated the field with cheap, easy-to-use maps of the whole of France, supplemented by their famous red hotel and restaurant guide, commonly known as *Le Guide Michelin*, and a series of 19 regional, green, tourist guides. The Michelin maps and guides are cleverly interconnected, e.g. towns underlined in red in the maps have entries in the red guide, every town and village featured in the red guide is referred back to the map and the green guide in which it is covered, and town plans in the red guide as well as the green guides coincide directly with the layout in the maps.

There are 44 detailed yellow Michelin road maps covering the whole country on a scale of 1/200,000. These are ideal for day-to-day motoring. They are remarkably good value for money, and include a mass of useful information, rather like Ordnance Survey maps. Their only failing is that they do not include contours, though the most recent editions do have shadings to indicate altitudes. In spite of this and the arrow markings on roads to indicate gradients in excess of 5%, one tends to overlook the ups and downs when route planning. If you own any of these unshaded, flat editions you should check whether an improved version has been published. Michelin maps are brought up to date and republished frequently, and we know from bitter experience that it is definitely unwise to use an out-of-date edition! From this point of view, it pays to buy Michelin maps in France, where one is less likely to find old stock and where the price is lower.

The red Michelin guide, issued annually, is a must for travellers at any level. It is published in French only, but has a multi-lingual introduction, and the explanatory symbols speak an international language. As a supplement to the Michelin maps it is important, but even on its own it is a vital source of information. It contains lists of recommended hotels and restaurants, which we have always found uncannily reliable over the years, information on the garage facilities in each town featured, as well as a short summary of the things of interest to be seen in that town, numbers of inhabitants, telephone and postal codes. The many town plans alone are quite invaluable in helping you to find your way through or about towns. All the important places like town hall, police station, post office, hospital and tourist office are indicated on these plans, as well as the exact location of the recommended hotels and restaurants.

It is basically on restaurant recommendations that the Guide Michelin has built its reputation. Every year its inspectors examine all existing recommendations as well as prospective new candidates, eliminating some and adding others, so the guide changes from year to year. To be entirely up-to-date on restaurant recommendations (the rest of the information does not change all that much) one needs a new guide every year. Imagine having gone out of your way to treat yourself to dinner in a 'two-star Michelin' listed in last year's guide to find, when you want to show it to your friends in their up-to-date guide, that it is no longer listed! Michelin's star-rating is generally well-known by now and is as follows:

1-star: very good cooking it its class . . . a good place to stop on your journey

2-stars: excellent cooking, worthy of a detour . . . do not expect such meals to be cheap

3-stars: . . . the best cooking in France, worthy of a special journey . . . one will pay accordingly

For rather more modest aspirations there is yet another rating: good meals at a modest price, indicted by a red 'R' against the hotel or restaurant entry. All other recommendations for hotels and restaurants are for general standards, facilities and comfort rather than food.

When it comes to concise, clearly presented information on the French regions, on landscape, historical and geological background, local flora, fauna and folklore, art, architecture and sights in general, the Michelin Green Guides are hard to beat and they are modestly priced. There are now 19 of these (including Corsica) covering the whole of France, though only seven of them are in English. Place entries are in alphabetical order, complemented by town plans, relief maps of localities to illustrate suggested itineraries, sketches of panoramas, sights and architectural features. The information given on opening hours of castles, museums and other public places of interest is invaluable when planning a day's activities. An amazing amount of information has been packed between the covers of these apparently modest books, priced at around £3.50. Even those which are not in English can be tackled quite well with a basic knowledge of French and the help of a good dictionary.

Undoubtedly the most detailed and comprehensive hardcover guides to France are the *Guides Bleues*, in French, published by Hachette and obtainable from Hachette's French Bookshop, 4 Regent Place, London W1R 6BH. The 17 volumes are fairly bulky compared to the green Michelin guides, but they are extremely thorough in their descriptions of towns, sites, monuments and itineraries and represent a standard library for the really serious traveller.

Also in French are three titles in the Jeune Afrique series: *La Bretagne*, *La Provence*, and *Val de la Loire*. These beautifully produced and illustrated books can only be bought in France.

Amongst the guide books to France published in the UK, *Fodor's Budget France* deserves mention. Naturally, a book of this nature which covers so much in one volume, lacks a lot of detail, but it gives a first-class idea of the country as a whole and an instant picture of each region.

Not a travel guide in the same sense but a perceptive, personal account of the history, geography, the people and the legends of the regions of the rivers, Lot, Dordogne and Tarn is Freda White's book Three River of France (Faber).

Of a rather different concept is Baedeker's France, published and distributed by the AA but also available from book sellers. It is essentially an A - Z gazetter of towns with a short section of practical information on motoring, shopping, language, weather etc.

More detailed and, to a large extent, rather academically orientated, are the Collins Companion Guides covering Paris, Normandy, S.W. France, Loire Valley and the South of France.

They are both informative and easy to read.

Anyone who likes his maps to show rather more detail than the Michelin yellow maps do will find the *Cartes Touristiques* of the IGN (Institut Géographique National) of great value. These green IGN maps are the equivalent of the Ordnance Survey maps in the UK and are published specifically as tourist maps. They have a scale of 1:100,000 (1 cm = 1 km), which is twice that of the Michelin yellow maps. Thus they contain many more small roads and footpaths and are really essential for the detailed investigation of a particular area. Their second advantage is that they are contoured and in full colour. However, they are more expensive, and their larger size and method of folding makes them more awkward to use in the car. There are 74 IGN Tourist maps covering the whole of France (including Corsica). Such maps can save you a lot of headaches when you decide to strike across country, for they will leave you in no doubt about the difficulty of the route you have chosen.

The IGN red series consists of 16 maps with tourist itineraries. They are in full colour and very clear, but have no contour lines. Their scale of 1:250,000 is slightly smaller than that of the yellow Michelin maps, which means that they are not as detailed, but they are very good for itinerary planning.

IGN publish a large number of other maps of rather more specific interest. No. 902 entitled *Principales richesses historiques et artistiques* (scale 1:1,000,000) shows at a glance the historic monuments and art treasures of France. Map No. 903 is of great interest to walkers, since it covers the *Sentiers du Grande Randonée* (long-distance hiking itineraries). Additionally, there are series of large-scale maps covering the regional and national nature parks, the mountain regions, the major forests, and the more important islands like Ré, Oléron and Noirmoutier. All the IGN maps can be obtained in the UK from IGN Maps (UK) Limited, 122 Kings Cross Road, London WC1X 9DS, who will also send a free catalogue and price list.

A large amount of exceptionally well-produced and informative tourist material can be obtained in the UK from the French Government Tourist Office and in France from the Regional Tourist Committees and the local tourist offices (see 'Advance Information', p.10). This includes brochures and maps on regions and towns, hotel and restaurant lists (see also

'Hotels', pp.29-37) lists of events, attractions and sports activities.

The French Ministry of Transport publishes annually, under the name of *Bison Futé* (Smart Buffalo), a map to help motorists through the holiday traffic. This publication (see also p.67) is handed to visiting motorists free on arrival at a French port or major customs post. Its forecast of the critical days of severe traffic density from mid-June to mid-September (which are different each year) is invaluable in avoiding the worst of the French holiday exodus traffic. It also gives details of roadworks in progress, how to negotiate difficult connurbations like Paris, Bordeaux, Lyon, Dijon, etc. and provides numbers to telephone for 24-hour traffic information. On the map itself are marked all the bottlenecks and the recommended alternative routes (*itinéraires bis*) which should be taken to avoid them. Also marked are 24-hour petrol stations and roadside information centres. These information centres, of which there are about 80 in the busiest traffic areas, are staffed by hostesses who can answer traffic queries, give information on hotels, camp sites, nearest garages or doctors, make telephone bookings and let you make urgent telephone calls to family members or friends. The *Bison Futé* map can be obtained in advance in the UK from the AA, to members only. We cannot stress too strongly that the information provided by *Bison Futé* should not be ignored.

Map reading — a small digression*

In a country as large as France a great deal of the enjoyment of motoring depends on being able to use maps well, so we make no excuse for saying a few words here about map reading and how it should be done. Most people will regard it as easy, a kind of skill which comes naturally, but years of experience have shown us

---

*To those readers who feel that we are trying to tell our Grandmother how to suck eggs, we apologise. Just skip this section and move on to more 'grown-up matters'. We have included it because we have met so many people who have found this aspect of motoring quite difficult, indeed so difficult that it has caused them endless arguments in the car. If we can be the cause of happier relationships on holiday and the means of more people getting to their true destinations on time, then we shall feel that we have fulfilled a long felt wish!

that this is not true. Many people map-read only with difficulty and then do not manage to take in all the information the map contains. A few hints, therefore, might not come amiss:

Firstly, orient the map correctly, using a compass if you have one. If not, use the well-known Boy Scout method of pointing the hour hand at the sun and halving the angle between it and 12 o'clock, which will give you, roughly, south. For the occasional briefing session in fine weather this can be done on the bonnet of the car, but for most of the hour-to-hour driving the passenger-cum-co-driver has to map-read 'on the wing' so to speak. A small board with a clip to hold the map open at the correct fold makes life easier, and since maps do not get any better by being scribbled on, a see-through plastic sheet or folder can be clipped over the map on which marks can be made with a chinagraph pencil.

Secondly, be sure to read the names on the map correctly against the features to which they refer. This may sound very obvious, but on a crowded map it is so easy to read the name of a village against the blob immediately to the right when it really refers to the blob immediately to the left. It helps a lot to use a magnifying glass.

Next, when working out the route ahead, check carefully whether a turn-off is to the *right* or the *left*. Confusion invariably arises when travelling north to south. While you are holding the map 'upside-down' nothing can go wrong, but as soon as you have to turn it back to 'normal' to be able to read the place names, it happens: you say 'left' when you should have said 'right', and before you spot your mistake you are several miles up the wrong road, while the map devil rubs his hands with glee!

Before giving instructions to the driver, count carefully the number of side roads before the turn-off, take into account any landmarks on the way and express yourself clearly, e.g. 'Take the second turning on the right, which is the D52 in the direction of XYZ. The turning is roughly 100m past a bridge over a railway line.' A little work done in advance will save a lot of argument later.

French roads are very well signposted, and on the maps we have mentioned all roads are clearly numbered at frequent intervals, but the French road numbering system can lead to momentary confusion when it comes to *routes départmentales*. Since D-roads are numbered within the *département*, any D-road will change its number as it passes across the border into another *département*, and unless you have figured this out in advance you will be baffled as you suddenly find yourself on the apparently wrong road through no fault of yours! Also, a D-road may change into an N-road (*route national*), or vice versa, without warning, and thereby change its number. Changes in road numbering and designation often occur in town centres: what looks, on superficial inspection of the map, like one and the same road just going straight through the town, may be one road going in and entirely another road coming out!

Ideally, map reading can be much more than just an instrument for travelling from A to B without getting lost. It can be a help when the driver wants to overtake ('In about another kilometer we'll come to a long stretch of dead-straight road') or when everyone wants to stop for lunch ('the next village looks large enough to have a baker's shop, and just the other side there is a small road leading down to the river . . .'). You can tell the children where the railway goes which you are just crossing, anticipate a view point (marked on the Michelin maps,) round the next bend, spot churches, castles, ruins, lakes, dams which might be worth a small detour.

Of course, there is one more thing about map reading which enlivens proceedings enormously: it is the commonest cause of argument between husband and wife! So why not train one of the children to do it.

3. PLANNING A TRIP

We have always had a great deal of fun out of planning a summer holiday during the winter and spring months. The exercise has two distinct functions. Firstly, it means that we work out carefully what is feasible in the time we have available. Secondly, we look closely at the costs and make a reasonable estimate based on what we can afford. Finally, we do our homework on what is to be seen *en route* and in the area we have chosen as our destination. This is, needles to say, far better than the all too common practice of looking things up after you have come back in order to find out just what you have seen!

Timing

The first stage is to make a day planner chart. This is simply a diary covering the number of days of the holiday on which we allocate the days devoted to the various stages of the holiday, i.e. from home to the other side, the journey down, time spent at destination, the journey home. At this stage we also discuss the times of ferries outward and inward.

The time of the ferry crossing is critical if you are to make a good start to the holiday. Depending on how far you have to travel to the channel port, it should be so chosen that you drive no more than your planned daily average even on the first day. In our case, living at Colchester and crossing from Dover, we reckon to make the crossing around midday, arriving in France early afternoon and spending the first night not more than three hours from Calais. An alternative, which we recommend only to the hardy, is to drive through the night when the traffic is light. In this case we would leave by a boat at about 10.00 p.m., arriving in France about midnight. Then, by taking the motorway to Paris and a bit beyond, it is possible to get well the far side of Paris before morning.

This is what we did two years ago when we took two children asleep in the back of our Volvo Estate and we actually arrived in the vicinity of Le Mans by about 8.00 a.m. Whilst this method does get you well on the way without too much difficulty, it does give you a problem the second day when tiredness tends to catch up with you rather suddenly.

After considerable experience of starting at all times of the day and frequently resorting to the night-time dash, we would recommend a relaxed start to the holiday as the best way to go about matters.

Planning the return crossing can be more difficult unless you allow a reasonable amount of time to get to the coast. Our experience is that it is infinitely better to make a relaxed return journey, arriving at the channel port at a time which will enable you to reach home by early evening on the same day. When booking the return, you can always take the option of an *open booking*, which will put you at risk for a place on the ship but gives you a certain flexibility in the last stages.

Before studying possible routes in any detail, we invariably do a cost estimate. This particular trip, in 1983, was based on the use of a *gîte* for the two weeks to be spent in the Cahors region, with hotels for the nights spent outward and inward. Costs have escalated in the meantime, but the principle is the same.

Costing

Firstly, we estimate the total milage we are likely to cover during the whole trip and calculate petrol consumption accordingly. Calais — Cahors is approximately 550 miles by the most direct route. We then added 900 miles for incidental motoring. In effect, we exceeded this figure by 20%, since we usually cover a fair bit more distance then we have bargained for. It is always as well to add this kind of figure to first estimates.

Our costing plan for 2 adults and 2 children aged 8 and 10 looked something like this:

	£
Cross Channel return fare car and 4 passengers	163.00
Green card insurance	18.00
Petrol	130.00
Travel Insurance	33.00
	344.00

Hotels en route, down, (3 nights)	580.00F	
Breakfasts	120.00	
Meals en route	400.00	
Lunches (picnic)	150.00	
Hire of *gîte* (2 weeks)	1000.00	
Food for two weeks	900.00	
Meals out	840.00	
Spending money (excl. children's pocket money)	300.00	
Hotels en route, back (2 nights)	380.00	
Meals en route	280.00	
Lunches (picnic)	100.00	
(rate of exchange in 1983: 11.70)	5,050.00F	432.00
Add for contingencies		100.00
		876.00

Planning the route

To do this you need a small-scale, but detailed, map of France (about 1:1,000,000) on which most small towns are included, together with the yellow Michelin maps covering the individual sections of the route. Select a route which appears fairly direct, then say to yourself: 'Is this the most interesting route? Could we, perhaps, have a more worthwhile drive down by deviating slightly from this route yet still not add too much to our mileage?' The chances are that a little investigation (and here you will need to refer to guide books like the green Michelin) will reveal that there is a more interesting route, which involves little extra mileage.

Plans 1/2

We then draw up two diagrammatic maps on sheets of plain paper. Not to scale, these simply give the mileages between important towns on route. If there are seemingly worthwhile detours at any point these are marked, and the mileage appended in the margin. Sometimes a completely different route for *part* of the journey seems desirable. This is also penned in. We use

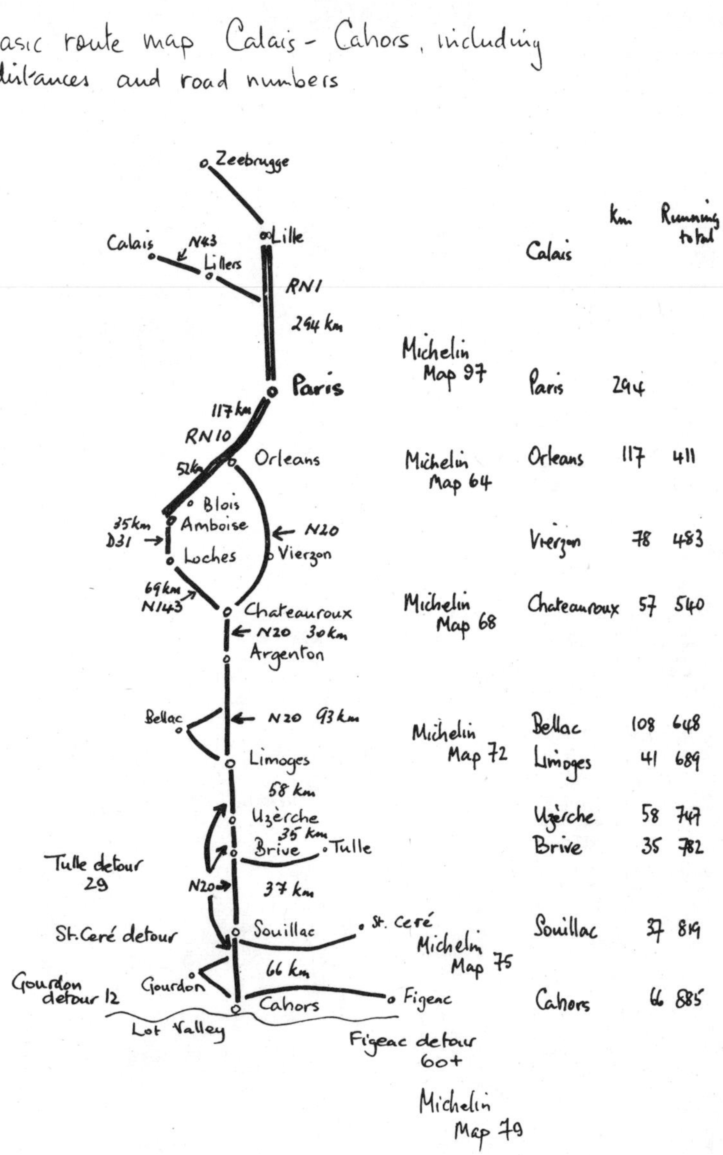

Plan 1: Example of a planned route

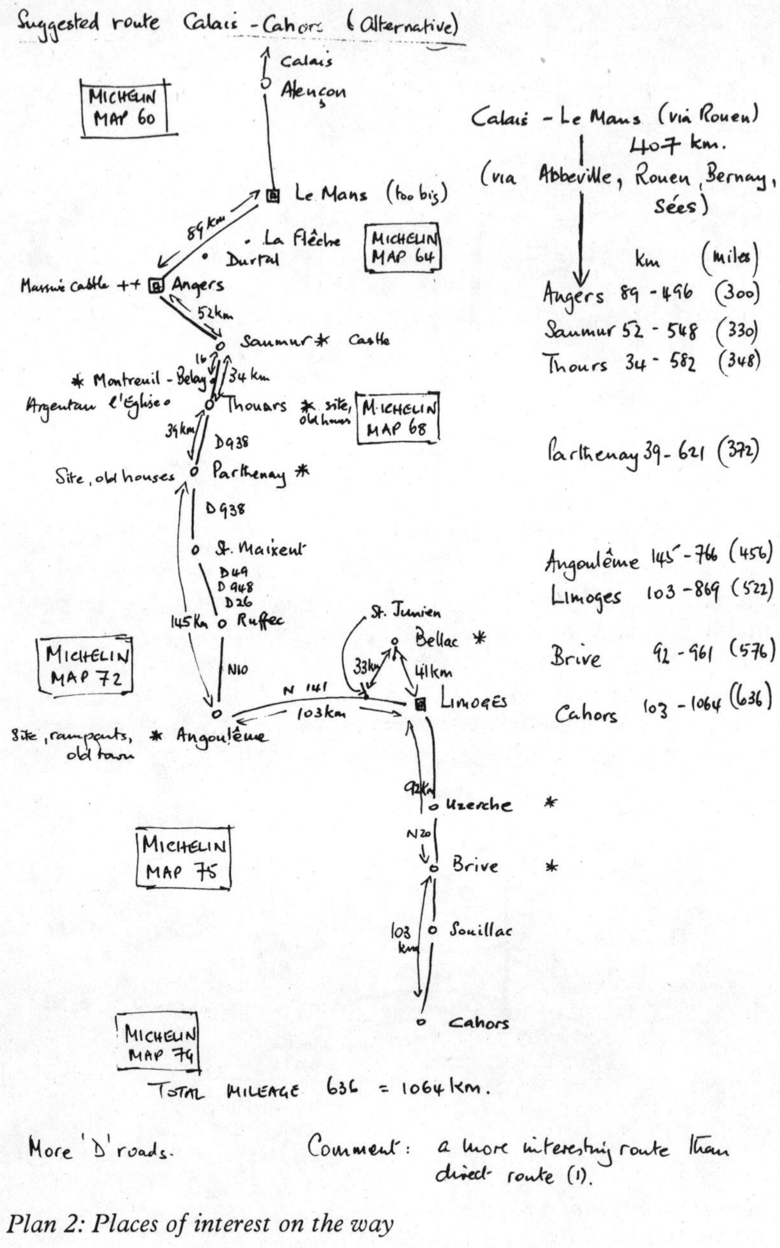

Plan 2: Places of interest on the way

coloured inks for the various things, black for the direct route, green for the detours, red for the mileages, etc. One of the sketch maps shows the planned route, while the other indicates the places of interest on the way, but both give the numbers of the Michelin maps needed to cover each section. Down one side of each sheet we normally write a summary of the mileages between the places marked. The road numbers are also clearly marked so that they can be picked up quickly by the navigator.

Plan 3

A third sketch map deals with hotel possibilities, gleaned from Michelin and other sources. In this we mark essential facts like costs of rooms, meal costs and whether the hotel is modern. This merely acts as a quick reference to possibilities, but can easily be digressed from.

On occasions we have expanded greatly on the amount of historical information available for the various towns, thus fixing in our minds what is really worth seeing, since we always regard the trip down as an integral part of the holiday and not just a chore to be got over as quickly as possible.

Doing this kind of planning means surrounding yourself with guides and maps long before departure. In this way you acquire a first class knowledge of their contents and shortcomings. You will also have a very good idea of what you can achieve in one day. We never reckon on spending less than one hour, perhaps more, in stopping to look at any ancient monument we have noted, and where a whole town is concerned we may spend up to two or three hours, depending on its size.

The exciting part about making itineraries is that it heightens your anticipation of the holiday and it saves you from blundering through the really exciting French countryside unaware of what you might be missing. Of course, depending on your degree of imagination, the reality may disappoint, but that is a chance you have to take.

What happens when we reach our destination? Well, we may have done some planning along the lines of the route maps down, but more likely we will simply have acquainted ourselves from guide books and brochures with the area as a whole, simply noting

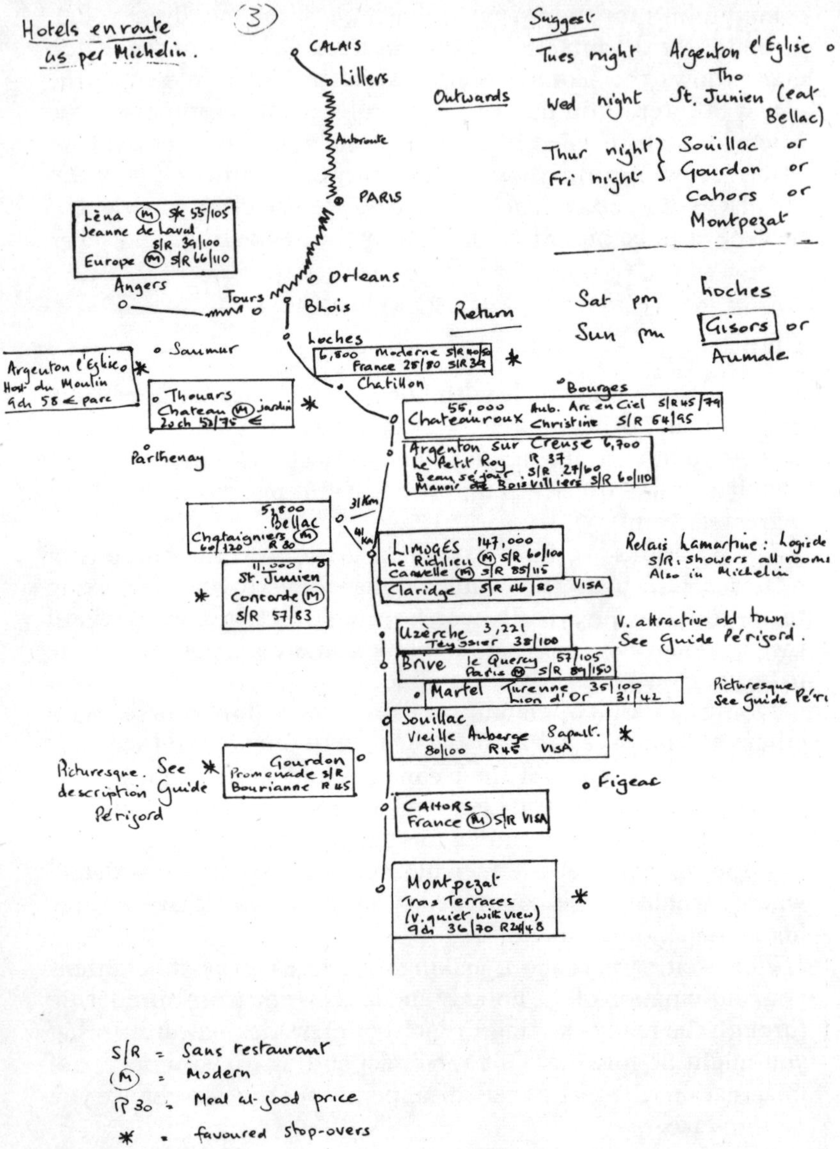

Plan 3: Overnight hotel possibilities on the way

down the main places of interest as a list and having a good look at the detailed map of the region. Then we will spend an hour over breakfast each day deciding what or what not to do. A good many days will be spent in the immediate neighbourhood, getting to know the local village and its people and not venturing more than a few kilometres, probably to get food and other essentials. Right at the beginning of a stay anywhere we make a point of going to the tourist office in the nearest town to get any useful information which we have not been able to collect in advance: brochures on the regions, lists of restaurants, addresses of doctors and hospitals, dentists, location of nearest swimming pool and other sports facilities, calendar of local events.

With or without children, it is not a bad idea to keep a detailed log and even a scrapbook of your progress. The scrapbook, especially, can contain all sorts of things, which in later years will stir the memory. Good postcards are often better than your own photographs, hotel bills recall the meals and the rooms you had, papers in which your *patisserie* or *charcuterie* was wrapped will bring back memories of what you ate, as will restaurant bills. Even tickets for bus rides, supermarket bills, visits to caves and bank exchange slips go in our scrapbooks. In between all the memorabilia you can write a short commentary.

The return trip, you will note, has not so far been mentioned. That is because that is a decision we like to reach after we have spent part of our holiday at the chosen destination. We will, certainly, have looked at alternative routes, sometimes even involving quite large detours. In the end we either go back via some of the places we enjoyed on the way down, just for a second look, or we take a moderately easy route nearly parallel to the route down, but enabling us to look at some other interesting things. We will plan this out on paper in the same way, do our homework on hotels and sites and then try to make the return journey a part of the holiday rather than a mad dash for the coast.

Of course we realise that this approach is not for everyone. Those who simply want the sun of the south will go there as fast as possible, spend as much time there as possible and then return with all haste. Sad, how much they miss of the more exciting parts of France.

4. ACCOMMODATION

Where do we stay?

Basically, holiday accommodation in France boils down to 5 main possibilities: Hotels, *gîtes ruraux*, private apartments, villas and campsites. In terms of cost, hotel accommodation is, of course, the most expensive, all the more so since it entails eating out at least once a day, either in the hotel's own restaurant or in one nearby. However, away from major tourist regions, and sometimes even in large towns, one does come across hotels which offer ridiculously cheap rooms, especially for family accommodation, which means one large room for a family of say four in two double-beds. The reason for the low price may be that the hotel has not modernised its rooms, or some of its rooms, or that a room is over a smelly kitchen, or a garage, or has no window. One very cheap room we came across not so long ago was illuminated only by a glazed panel in the door!

When you arrive late and tired and only want an overnight stay such things matter much less than they would if you had to put up with them for a fortnight. Surprisingly, though, such hotels often have very good and even famous restaurants and, having given you a room for practically nothing, expect you to eat there, so that you pay on the roundabouts what you haven't paid on the swings.

Gîtes ruraux, (simple country holiday houses), of which there are literally thousands in rural areas all over France, are surprisingly reasonable. In fact for a family a *gîte* at the lower end of the price-range is not very much more costly than an expensive 4-star campsite, and you don't have to share the grounds and the showers with 200 other people! The prices and standards of comfort of *gîtes* are governed by the administrating association.

An *appartement meublé*, or simply *un meublé*, on the other hand, which is not labelled a *gîte*, is simply a private furnished flat which, although officially graded for comfort under the *normes* of the *Charte Nationale des Meublés Saisonniers*, is not bound by a fixed price and prices are not quoted in lists, so that the proprietor can charge you what he likes at the time. The other difference is that of site: *gîtes* are always out in the country, whereas *meublés* are mainly found in, or on the edge of, towns.

The most comfortable, and most expensive type of furnished accommodation is probably one of the many villas, some of them decidedly luxurious, which can be rented through the various villa hire organisations in this country and elsewhere. If you want to hire a manor house in a 6-acre park or have a private swimming pool and tennis court you should contact a few of these villa companies. Their selection, incidentally, is not usually limited to luxury villas, some offer simple cottages, too.

It is probably true to say that camping is more a matter of addiction than economy, but that does not detract from the fact that it is still the cheapest way of spending a holiday in France. On the other hand, the growing spread of low-priced *gîte* accommodation has considerably narrowed the price-gap between accommodation *en plein air* and that in four stone walls. The weather (especially south of the Loire), the scenery and the availability of well-equipped camp sites everywhere have made France a camping country *par excellence*. Inevitably, the news has travelled, with the result that in July and August one needs to have the gregarious mentality of an ant and the space requirements of a canned sardine to survive on some of the overflowing camp sites in the more popular tourist regions, notably the Mediterranean coast, the Atlantic coast south of Bordeaux and the Bois de Boulogne outside Paris!

A Way with Hotels

To book or not to book, that is the question. The answer depends largely on when, where and how long you want to stay. One reason for not booking a longer stay in advance is that you may not like it at all when you get there. If you have made your booking in writing from the UK you cannot get out of it by simply driving away and booking into the hotel down the road, which is much nicer. Having paid a deposit does not release you from your legal obligation to pay part or all of the balance due if the proprietor does not re-let your room(s). However, if you travel in July or August and especially if you intend to stay in a hotel in a popular holiday area for more than just the odd night, you are taking a big risk by not booking in advance.

A good deal of guess-work can be taken out of advance booking by choosing a hotel which belongs to a chain or group which is known for the consistency of its standards (see 'Hotel Groups and Chains', p.34). Several of these groups have booking services in the UK and other countries, which makes things much easier, and some publish an illustrated brochure to help with the choice.

The Red Michelin guide is always reliable for its choice of hotels and offers the advantage that it includes town plans for all the larger towns as well as the smaller, touristically popular places, on which recommended hotels are marked. It is, after all, important to know whether your hotel is on a main road, in the old town, near the railway or miles from anywhere. The French Government Tourist Office in London (see p.10 and address list p.185) stocks hotel lists and town plans of many of the popular places. It also publishes, as part of its annual fact-sheet, a list of hotel groups with UK booking offices. For personal callers only, the FGTO has a photo-file with illustrations of many hotels. Bookings other than those with UK booking offices can be made through departmental *Loisirs-Accueil* offices in France (see p.10 and address list pp.187-189).

In the off-season, i.e. before July and after mid-September, it is quite safe to set off un-booked and look around when you get to your destination. If you invest in the red Michelin guide and also collect a good selection of hotel lists in advance, you can spend several enjoyable evenings beforehand making a short list of likely possibilities. This will allow you to make a bee-line for them on arrival. If one hotel has no vacancies, another very likely will.

If you come completely unprepared and undocumented it is very important that you should arrive at your destination early in the day and go straight to the local *Syndicat d'Initiative* or *Office de Tourisme* and ask for a hotel list and possibly some help with it. You can then plan to look around at leisure.

Most *Syndicats* close for lunch, from 12 noon till 2 p.m. or 2.30 p.m. and most of them will be open till 5.30 p.m. Beyond that, you cannot tell. Some close on Monday afternoon, some Wednesday afternoon, some Saturday afternoon. Some, in very busy tourist centres, are even open on Sundays in the season. Here again the indispensable red Michelin guide will enlighten you!

In July and August it is definitely not safe to adopt such a casual attitude. We have never yet failed to find a bed for the night even at the height of the season, but have had many cliff-hangers through starting the search much too late in the day. It is absolutely essential to arrive at a hotel early in the day, say after lunch, preferably by 2 p.m. but certainly not later than 4 p.m. Even arriving at 5 p.m. we have often been told the unwelcome news that the last room had been 'let 5 minutes ago', and by 7 p.m. we have gratefully accepted a suite at a luxury hotel at five times the budgeted price as an attractive alternative to sleeping in the car! Some of the larger, well-organised hotels, especially those belonging to a chain, will be very nice about it and make suggestions about where to try next, or even make a 'phone call on your behalf, but we have seen too many worn and anxious-looking families propped up against reception counters to believe that this kind of brinkmanship enhances the enjoyment of your holiday.

If you have several one-night stops to arrange it may be a good idea to stay in a hotel belonging to a group or chain (see p.34) which offers a booking service within the chain. This means that the receptionist will, usually free of charge, make a telephone or telex booking for the following night in another hotel belonging to the chain. For example, if you spend the night at the Novotel in Amiens you can have your room at the Novotel in Blois booked before you leave in the morning, after you have consulted the map to compare distances with your and your family's likely stamina that day.

There are several endearing aspects to French hotels. One is the proprietor's or receptionist's readiness to show you a room (if there is one vacant) before you decide to take it. No sooner have you asked than they will grab a key or two off the hook and motion you towards the stairs with an enthusiastic '*Vous voulez voir la chambre?*' (Do you want to see the room?) No trouble at all, it seems, and if you decide not to take it — well, *tant pis* (too bad). The effort of climbing up all those stairs is simply part of a day's work. It is definitely advisable to follow the invitation to see the room, especially in older hotels, because you may not like it at all, and there is no point in being timid about it.

Another helpful and comforting feature is the legal obligation to display a room price list where everybody can see it. This may be on the wall in the hall or behind the receptiopn desk, or on the reception desk, or even in a window by the door. It lists every room in the hotel by room number, basic facilities (i.e. *lavabo*, *douche*, *bain*) and price per room per night. The room price is also displayed in the room itself, usually on the inside of the door. Note that the price is per room, not per person, unless otherwise agreed. There may be two prices for some rooms, depending on how many people sleep in it. For example, a room with a double and a single bed may cost 180F if occupied by two persons, and 210F if occupied by three. Or a separate price may be listed for a *lit supplémentaire*, i.e. an extra bed, in any room that can take one. Beware! If two of you occupy two beds, one double and one single you will be charged as though three people had occupied the room.

Most hotels will be very accommodating in putting extra beds for children into the parents' room. Even if the room is on the small side, they will obligingly try to squeeze another two folding beds in, if *you* don't mind. Or if they have run out of folding beds, and you happen to have a camp bed or air mattress with you, a family hotel (not the Carlton in Cannes!) will usually let you use your own, if you suggest that this might solve your problem for the night, and charge you nothing extra, especially if you provide your own sleeping bag or bedding. For this reason alone it is a good idea, if you travel with children, to take at least one air mattress or camp bed and a sleeping bag. But for this precaution we, or our two children, would have had an uncomfortable night on several occasions when the only room left at a hotel was a double room with one extra folding bed.

Beware of the type of double bed (*grand lit*) which is still found in many of the older hotels. In all the many years we have travelled in France we have never come across one (well, maybe one or two) which did not have a mattress that was so well worn in the centre that one had to hang on to the outer edge all night to avoid slithering inexorably down into the central depression. You will get up in the morning feeling as though you had spent the night in a hammock. People who sleep habitually in hammocks may claim that this is the pinnacle of sleep comfort, but most conventional sleepers will find it hard on the the back. So, if the hotel gives you a choice of a double room with either *grand lit* or *lits jumelés* (twin beds), it might be better to go for the latter, or simply *deux lits*, if the room description lists them as such.

Breakfast is hardly every included in the room price of French hotels. Where it is, perhaps as part of a *forfait* arrangement (all-in price), the price list displayed at the reception or the hotel list from which you are working, should say so. In the red Michelin guide, for example, room prices inclusive of breakfast are indicated by a coffee-cup symbol following the number of rooms and preceding the min./max. price, i.e. 22ch/symbol/85/120. It is always safer to ask whether breakfast is included. In any event, whether breakfast is included in the room price or not, you are not obliged to take it and the hotel may not charge you for it (see p. 137 for alternatives to hotel breakfast).

Hotel categories

There are, basically, two categories of hotel in France: the *hôtels de tourisme* and the *hôtels non homologués de tourisme*. Hotels in the first category, i.e. 'Tourist Hotels' are graded annually by the French Ministry of Leisure and each, according to comfort, amenities and the standard to which it is kept, allotted one, two, three, or four stars. There is no five-star grading, in theory, but the 'four-star L' grading for luxury hotels amounts to as much. This grading in itself does not imply narrowly fixed prices, so that minimum and maximum room prices of two hotels in the same star category may differ considerably. For example, the cheapest room in one 3-star hotel may be 65F, whereas in another it is 190F. It all depends on the specific comfort of the particular room and also on the situation and popularity rating of the particular hotel.

Most hotels listed in official hotel lists, published by local or regional tourist offices, are *hôtels de tourisme*, whose grading can be relied on. *Hôtels non homologués* are outside this official grading. They are normally comparably to, or lower than a 1-star rating, and a leaflet published by the French Trade and Prices Office comments that 'generally their standard of comfort is lower, but their prices are lower'. This does not mean that one could not safely stay at such a hotel and be very well looked after, or that these hotels are not run to a very acceptable standard.

The *Auberges de France*, for example, which are part of the well-known chain of *Logis de France* hotels, are *non homologués*, many of them because they are too small. More is said about them in the section on 'Hotels chains and groups'.

An *hôtel de tourisme* can be recognized on the outside by a blue enamel plaque, pinned to the wall, stating 'Hôtel de Tourisme' and more often than not 'NN'. 'NN' means *nouvelles normes*, i.e. 'new standards', which are, by official definition 'more exacting than the old ones and ensure greater comfort'. The blue plaque should also display the current year; if it does not, you should check that the star-grading indicated on the plaque is still up-to-date.

It is worth knowing, by the way, that in the red Michelin guide hotels with 'modern amenities' are signalled by the symbol [M] after the name of the hotel. This very often means, in fact, that the hotel is altogether of fairly recent construction.

Hotel Groups and Chains

There are now so many hotel chains and groups in France, some of them international, that one would not dream of listing them all. In some cases, the fact that a hotel belongs to a group has no practical implications for you as the customer other than that the hotel can be expected to adhere to the group charter in the standard of amenities and service it offers and that you can complain to a central administrative office if you are dissatisfied. In other cases there can be additional advantages. For example:

> Some groups have a booking service in the UK, which makes advance booking very convenient. A list of these is available from the French Government Tourist Office in London (for address see p.185).
>
> Groups publish their own lists which feature addresses, descriptions and sometimes illustrations of all member hotels. These can, sometimes, be obtained from travel agents or the French Government Tourist Office, but certainly from the group's administrative offices or any member hotel.
>
> In some groups the hotel at which you are staying will make a telephone or telex reservation, free of charge, to another hotel in the same group for your next stop.

Here are some of the better-known hotel groups:

Logis de France et Auberges de France. Thousands of small to medium-sized, family-run hotels all over France, mostly outside urban centres, belong to this group. The aims of the group are to offer not only comfortable accommodation with modern amenities and simple, well-prepared family cooking, but to give guests a personal, friendly welcome. *Logis* are one- or two-star graded tourist hotels. *Auberges* are simpler, and usually smaller, and therefore do not qualify to be graded as tourist hotels. Their sanitary facilities, as set out in the group's brochure, are minimal but adequate: running hot and cold in all rooms, communal bathroom with shower, bidet and washbasin, and communal WC. One of the special aims of member hotels of this group is to include authentic regional dishes in their menus.

The complete annual list of *Logis et Auberges de France* can be obtained from the French Government Tourist Office in London (address p.185) in return for a fee of 50p in stamps to cover postage and packing.

France Accueil. This is a hotel chain of 160 hotels, all 2- or 3-star and owner-run, which put emphasis on tradition, comfort and regional cooking. They welcome pets, which is good news for non-UK visitors who do not have to worry about quarantine rules, and they offer a free booking service (within the same *département* or to any adjacent *département*) from one hotel to any other hotel in the group. *France Accueil* hotels have a UK booking service: Minotels, 11 Palmeira Mansions, Church Road, Hove, East Sussex, Tel. 0273 731908, from which a list is available. There is no uniformity about *France Accueil* hotels; each is different and run along individual lines; some are old, some new, and so on.

*Novotel**. As the name implies, these are all modern hotels, which is a useful thing to be able to rely on for anyone who values modern hotels for their convenience and sophistication, i.e. features like large picture windows, sunblinds, wall-to-wall

---

*The distribution of *Novotels*, *Mercure* hotels and *Ibis* hotels is shown on a map '*La France du voyage*', obtainable from Sofitel, 16 Berkeley Street, London W1X 5EA.

carpeting, tasteful sanitary ware and television in bedrooms. Novotels are all three- or four-star hotels run along fairly uniform lines and consistently high standards. Most of them are just outside the larger towns (including Paris), easily accessible and with plenty of parking, which makes them ideal for overnight stops. While some Novotels are in rather sober surroundings, near airports or among peripheral high-rise apartments, others are so pleasantly situated that they make the perfect base for a longer stay. For example, the one at Amboise (Loire), which stands in an elevated position, has a privileged view over the town, the river and the castle, the one at Le Touquet stands right on the beach, and so does the one at Île d'Oléron (Charente-Maritime).

Novotels are the answer for families with up to two children who value top standards and an easy-going atmosphere, but do not want to strain their budget. All *Novotels* offer to accommodate up to two children (under 12) free of charge in their parents' room, and since the rooms are spacious 4-bed rooms, this causes no problems in practice. A typical inclusive price for a double room at a *Novotel* (in 1983) might be 230F per night. There are a few which, due to the exceptional situation, popularity, facilities etc. (e.g. Le Touquet) are quite a bit more expensive. Current prices are best found in the red Michelin guide, which lists *Novotels* almost without exception. Every *Novotel* has a garden, a swimming pool and a play area for children, which is exactly what you and children want when you arrive stiff and weary on a hot afternoon. There is a bar/coffee bar which is open all day and an informal restaurant which serves very acceptable food, mainly of the grill variety, from a standard menu till late at night. Little extras make you feel that somebody really cares for your happiness; sachets of bubble-bath in the bathroom, a sewing kit from reception, the offer of a razor if you have forgotten yours, animal-shaped menu cards which children can keep and colour in. There is a free telex reservation service between all *Novotels* which is efficient, speedy and friendly. We have kept one Telex to prove it: it was sent from the *Novotel* at Blois to the *Novotel* at Amiens, and it concludes with the two receptionists wishing each other a 'Happy Day'! *Novotel* have a UK booking service: Sofitel, 16 Berkeley Street, London W1X 5EA, Tel. 01-499 0734, from which a detailed list of member hotels is available.

Ibis Hotels★. This chain covers over 60 two-star hotels on the outskirts of larger towns and tourist centres all over France. Their aim is to 'provide quality service at budget prices'. *Ibis* hotels are all modern, and although many of them suffer from a very unromantic situation (for example on peripheral housing or industrial estates) they make ideal motor hotels for reasonable one-night stays. They all have a restaurant which serves meals until 10.30 at night, while breakfast is served from 6 a.m. at a self-service buffet, which is very handy for a quick getaway in the morning. Children under 8 are accommodated free if they share their parents' room.

Ibis Hotels have no UK reservation service. A list is available and bookings can be made through Ibis (Head Office) Autoroute A6, CE 1406, 91019 Evry Cedex.

Inter-Hotels. This is an international hotel chain which in all parts of France alone covers over 200 two- and three-star hotels. *Inter-Hotels* are all up-to-date and run to very high standards. Their style is individual; each one is different: some are modern, some traditional, some elegant, some rustic. Nearly all of them are conveniently situated for sight-seeing and longer stays, in or near centres of large towns and popular resorts. *Inter-Hotel* publish an illustrated brochure of their hotels in France which can be obtained from Inter-France Reservations, 35 Harrington Gardens, London SW7, Tel. 01-373 2306, through whom reservations can be made. Reservations can also be made from one *Inter-Hotel* to another.

*Mercure Hotels**. This is a chain of about 40 three-star hotels, mainly in the north and east of France, all of them modern and with a high standard of comfort. Some are in town centres, including Paris, some outside towns. Most of them have a swimming pool, terrace, gardens, play area and a restaurant open until midnight. Children are accommodated free of charge in their parents room (in 3- or 4-bedded rooms, if no extra bed has to be provided). One noteworthy feature of *Mercure* hotels is the fact that most of them have rooms for handicapped people.

Mercure publish an illustrated list of their hotels, with prices quoted, which can be obtained from and bookings made through Sofitel, 16 Berkeley Street, London W1X 5EA. Tel. 01-400 0734. There is also a free reservation service from one *Mercure* hotel to another.

Gîtes Ruraux de France

A *gîte* (pronounced approximately like the English word 'sheet'), according to the dictionary, is 'a home, a resting place, a place to lay one's head', and this describes the spirit behind the idea very well. A *gîte* is supposed not only to be a restful place in the country, but also a home from home, and the person who lets it to you is expected to take a personal, benevolent interest in you. The official definition of a *Gîte Rural de France* is: reasonably priced, privately owned, self-catering accommodation, nearly always in a rural area of France, which has to meet the standards laid down by the charter of the Fédération Nationale des Gîtes Ruraux de *France*. This non-profit making organisation was set up in 1955 under the auspices of several French Ministries, including the Ministry of Agriculture and the Ministry of Tourism, with the aim of furthering tourism in rural France. The popularity of the *gîte* as a way of spending a self-catering budget holiday in close proximity with the French way of life has increased in recent years, not only with foreign visitors, especially the Dutch and the English, but with the French themselves.

We started hiring *gîtes* in the early seventies and have stayed in some *gîte* or other nearly every summer since. It could be said that a *gîte* becomes an addiction. Even if you have not been quite so lucky with your chosen *gîte* one year, and you swear that this has been the last time and you'll take the family to a luxury hotel in Funchal next year instead, you always come home with the gratifying feeling that you have made tremendous progress in getting to know the French and their way of life. And by the time the following spring comes round you find yourself once again flicking through the pages of the illustrated *gîtes* handbook in search of your dream cottage.

What can you expect when you hire a gîte?

Gîtes come in many shapes and sizes. A *gîte* may be a flat in a modern house on a hillside, built by the owner for his own use, or a restored stone cottage in a vineyard, or a hunting lodge in the grounds of an estate, or a converted outbuilding on a farm, or a terraced house in a small village. When the official description says that all *gîtes* are simple and adequate it means just that. Only very exceptionally, and then only in the top category of *gîte*, would you find a carpet or a mat on the floor. In all the years of staying in *gîtes* we have only once had a comfortably armchair to sit in! This spartan simplicity is perfectly logical when you consider that you are meant to live as the locals do and that the locals in a farming community do live very simply. If the owner of your *gîte* is a farmer or village artisan, his own living room will very probably be no more luxurious than the one in the *gîte* which he lets to you. In fact, many, if not most, *gîtes* do not have a separate living room at all but a large kitchen with a sitting and dining area. This, too, is quite typical of rural households, where all the everyday living takes place in the kitchen. The kitchen is almost invariably very well equipped, reflecting the important part that eating plays in France. Cookers are mostly large and modern, usually run on bottled gas, and there is always a good refrigerator and provision for plenty of hot water either from a gas geyser or an electric immersion heater. The variety of gadgets varies. It is never the same from one *gîte* to another, but the electric coffee grinder and the hand-operated lettuce 'spin-drier' seem to be ubiquitous. Certain essential items are sometimes present and sometimes not. In all our years of staying in *gîtes* we have never once found a washing-up brush and only twice an electric iron. The washing-up brush is no problem, we just bring our own. As for the iron, you should not hesitate to ask the owner of the *gîte* to supply you with one, because the charter states that 'household facilities must be available to help tenants wash and iron their clothes and house linen'.

The charter lays down in some detail all the mimimum requirements to which a place which has been registered as a *Gîte de France* must conform. For example:

— it must have electric light in all rooms, washing facilities consisting at least of a shower and washbasin, a sink with running water, an inside flush lavatory, and shutters or curtains on all windows.
— the place must be kept clean and in a perfect state of hygiene and painted regularly.
— inside fittings, fixtures and furniture must be in good condition and maintained as such.
— a minimum of furniture must be in each room, i.e. a full-size bed, a table, two chairs, a wardrobe and a closet in each bedroom; a cupboard, table and chairs in the living

room or area; fixtures necessary for a family, cooking facilities (coal, gas or electricity), a sink and a closet in the kitchen or kitchen area; and, in mountainous regions, a means of heating.

— shopping must be made easy for clients, by all useful means.
— the house front must be decorated with care and good taste.
— the surroundings must be neat and have, where possible, a quiet area and a play spot for children.
— the place should be completely cleaned and ventilated after each tenancy, and the welcoming of new tenants should be carried out by the owner or a person authorized by him.
— the price of the rental must include limited quantities of water, electricity and cooking facilities (i.e. coal, gas, etc.)

As far as this last provision is concerned, which entails that water, gas and electricity in excess of the allowed quantities must be paid for by the tenant, it must be said that in practice this happens very rarely. At least, it has never happened to us. Not a single one of our *gîte* owners has ever checked the electricity or water meter prior to our departure, nor has an owner ever flinched at replacing an empty gas bottle by a full one. It seems that on the whole owners rely on tenants being reasonable consumers. You would have to stand under the shower all day or heat the house by electricity to exceed the allowance of 500 litres of water per day and 4 kw/h electricity per day. As for the gas bottle, it is usually half empty from the previous tenant and nobody knows exactly how much he used and how much you did.

Heating, on the other hand, usually has to be paid for separately, especially if it is by oil. In the lowlands of France, and more particularly in the southern half of the country, you would not normally expect to need any heating in the summer, but at high altitudes it turns surprisingly cool in the evenings or if the weather is bad. One summer when we were enshrouded in cold, clammy clouds for several days at an altitude of 3,000 ft we had to keep the wood-burning stove in the kitchen going almost continuously. The large pile of wood provided by the owner, who had obviously foreseen this sort of weather, dwindled rapidly, but he refused to charge us for heating at the end of our stay (feeling, presumably, that we had suffered enough through the inclemency of the weather).

The requirement that the *gîte* should be completely cleaned and ventilated after each tenancy concerns, strictly speaking, the proprietor of the *gîte*, or whoever looks after it, and not the tenant. Nowhere in the (standard) rental contract have we ever found a clause that committed the tenant to undertake the cleaning of the *gîte* at the end of his stay, but we have come across one or two owners who made a point of stressing that they would appreciate it very much if we could leave everything *propre*.

In all fairness to the owner, the tenant should make an effort to leave the place in a reasonably clean and tidy condition without actually doing a spring-cleaning job. In the season especially, one let may finish at noon on Saturday and the next begin at 4 p.m. the same day, which leaves the owner, or more likely his wife, very little time in which to swing a mop and bucket, empty dustbins, replace gas bottles, air blankets and so on. If he is a working farmer, the owner and his family may be very busy getting in the hay or the corn before a spell of bad weather. On such occasions he has to depend entirely on the co-operation of his tenants in keeping his *gîte* in a respectable condition.

So if you ever come across a *gîte* that is less than spotless, try to think about it that way. On the other hand, if the place is revoltingly dirty and neglected you should complain to the owner immediately you set foot in it, and also, in writing or in person, to the *Relais Départemental des Gîtes de France* responsible for the particular department. Such action is not very likely to be necessary, but since this is an imperfect world, it is not entirely out of the question. We once had to move out of *gîte* in a great hurry because the mattresses turned out to be infested by bed bugs. Since this is something you only find out when you actually sleep in a bed, the representative of the *Relais Départemental* on his annual inspection is not likely to notice it. If nobody complain, the owner himself (in this case he was a farmer living several miles away) is not aware of it, either, so keeping quiet does no-one a favour.

On another occasion the interior of a *gîte* we had hired in some wooded hills had obviously not be redecorated for years. At an altitude of some 3,000 ft a great deal of heating was needed, especially since that particular *gîte* was also used for winter sports. The smoke from the wood burner in the kitchen had stained the ceiling and walls dark brown. The mildew on the walls of the bathroom, which faced north, did not help, either, but otherwise the place was clean and adequately equipped.

What do you do when faced with that sort of situation, when you feel you just cannot bear the thought of living in the place for a fortnight and all you want to do is get into the car and drive away? The answer really depends on the time of year. In the off-season, when it is not too difficult to find alternative accommodation, you could make a stand, tell the owner and the *Relais Départemental* what you think and, if your complaints are really well-founded, be released from your contract. If you have paid a deposit you will very likely lose that, and if you cannot convince the owner of the validity of your complaint you have to visit the office of the *Relais Départemental*, which may be quite a long drive away. To add to your problems it will not be open on a Saturday, and since this is likely to be a Saturday (standard lets being from Saturday to Saturday) you will not be able to do anything until Monday.

Our advice is to breathe deeply, especially in July and August, take stock of all the good aspects of the *gîte* and decide to put up with it, because the inconvenience you are causing yourself and your family in starting to look for somewhere else to stay may be considerable. The *Relais Départemental* will probably be quite unable to find you an alternative *gîte* in the same or even adjoining *département*, and after countless telephone calls, much teeth-sucking and visits to local Tourist Offices you will end up in an expensive hotel, because that is the only place left to go. On the other hand, if you decide to make the best of the *gîte* you will probably end up having a wonderful time after all. The owner and his family will turn out very friendly and helpful people (their kitchen may be as stained as yours) who ask you in for drinks and offer you farm produce for practically nothing. The children will make inseparable friends with dogs, cats, cows and ducks, the surrounding countryside will be delightful and, depending on which part of France you are staying in, will yield bonuses in the shape of raspberries and bilberries, mushrooms, fossils to collect, unusual birds and insects to watch. If the weather is fine you will not spend all that much time actually inside the *gîte*, and on the whole you will probably be rewarded in many ways for putting up with a measure of imperfection.

Perhaps it is fair to say that *gîtes* are not generally for the timid or the uncompromising, but for the enterprising and the bold. You may find yourself living miles from anywhere, in the middle of a field with no neighbours except members of the animal kingdom. You may find toads living outside the front door or hornets in a tree behind the house. If you live in a village or hamlet you may have chickens walking in through the door and the smell of cows, pigs and ducks wafting in through every window. Your landlord or landlady will want to talk to you (in French, Oh horror!) and explain how things work and you, even if you do not plan to go to the extent of discussing world politics with them, will probably have frequent cause to talk to them, if only to ask for a new light bulb or to enquire about the day for the rubbish collection. Anyone with even a fair command of French who is prepared to put it boldly into action will soon find that the landlord and his family and neighbours will be only too keen to talk and listen. Much useful local information one can obtain in this way and, after a while, people who seemed very aloof will start telling you about themselves. Asking them about their children is one certain way of getting the conversation flowing. The farmer who told us about his son having a doctor's practice in Limoges and being married to a German girl who goes Morris-dancing in Fort William is typical of a country parent who takes pride in his children having escaped the confines of a farming existence to follow more challenging and lucrative careers. It is, of course, this very drift away from the country, the dwindling rural populations and deserted houses, which prompted the French government in the first place to launch the *gîte* project as a means of giving country areas a new and lucrative part to play.

Classification of gîtes

As hotels are classified by stars, so *gîtes* are classified by ears of corn (*épis*). The *épi* is merely a basis for comparing one *gîte* to another and cannot be related to hotel categories. Since *gîtes* do not claim to be anything more than simple, congenial accommodation for country lovers, a *3-épis gîte* can in no way be compared for comfort to a 3-star hotel. Even a *3-épis gîte* may turn out to be very basic indeed. Officially, the definitions are:

1 *épi*: simple and convenient
2 *épis*: comfortable
3 *épis*: very comfortable

The reasons for classifying a *gîte* one way or the other are manifold and by no means rely on the quality of the mattresses only. The *Relais Départemental*, in classifying a *gîte*, takes into account the situation and accessibility of the place, whether it is isolated or close to a village or even a small town, whether it is detached or terraced, whether it is equipped with any furniture and fittings that exceed the very basic needs, whether the furniture is new, old, stylish or higgledy-piggledy, whether the house has a nice garden, terrace, garage etc. In many cases the difference between *gîtes* in adjacent categories may be purely theoretical. We stayed in one *3-épis gîte* which was superior to the *2-épis gîte* from which we had just come simply because it was situated in a much frequented beauty spot. In fact, the kitchen in the *2-épis* was a separate room and altogether much better, and so was the shower. (Note: it is much more common to find a shower in a *gîte* than it is to find a bath tub.) On the other hand, the previous year we had occupied a *3-épis gîte* which was a positive gem. The owner, a local vintner, had lovingly converted it from an ancient barn and furnished it for his own use. Its situation in a vineyard complemented the shady terrace, the barbecue, the antique furniture and the beautiful kitchen. The determining factor here was the price: it was the same size as but almost twice the price of the other *3-épis gîte*. In other words: category is not the only criterion. It must be read in connection with the price quoted.

The price of a gîte
The price you have to pay for a *gîte* depends on several factors:

its category (1-, 2-, or 3-épis), as discussed above
its size (accommodating anything from 2 to 8 persons)
its 'luxury' rating within its category
the time of year
the region

Generally, the price level, and the quality, of *gîtes* is higher in very popular, much frequented areas, especially in the mountains and by the sea (e.g. Finistère, Haute Savoie, Côte d'Azur) than it is in less frequented, touristically less well-known areas (e.g. Burgundy, Franche-Comté, Deux Sèvres). Also, the price difference between high and low season is more marked in areas which, because of their climate, get a tremendous influx of holidaymakers during two or three months in the summer, but are not very attractive at other times. For example, the coasts of Brittany and the northern Atlantic coast.

In a cheaper area (in 1983) a 2- or 3-épis *gîte* for 4 to 6 persons may cost between 300F and 600F in the low season, between 500F and 800F in the high season.

In an expensive area the price may be between 450F and 950F in the low season and between 650F and 1200F in the high season. These prices are per *gîte* per week. 'High season' means July and August, which are the traditional school holiday months, plus, in winter sports areas, December to April. All other months are low season, except that some *gîtes* charge slightly more in June and September.

As mentioned earlier, the price for a *gîte* includes adequate quantities of gas, water and electricity but not, in most cases, heating, bed and table linen, and breakages. Sometimes linen can be hired from the owner, but this should always be arranged in advance in writing. Our advice is to take your own if you can possibly find room for it in the boot.

How to book a gîte

Booking on the spot

If you intend to have a holiday in France in the off-season, say before mid-June or after mid-September, if you enjoy speaking French and finding your way about French towns in search of booking offices and, above all, if you like the excitement of uncertainty and last-minute decisions, you can choose the do-it-yourself approach and do nothing about booking a *gîte* until you actually get to France. Each département has a *Gîte de France* administrative office, the *Relais Départemental*, and many *départments* now have *Loisir-Accueil* offices (see p.10), which have a complete lists of *gîtes* available in the *département* and will make bookings. The address of the *Relais Départemental des Gîtes*

Ruraux de France can be obtained from any *Syndicat d'Initiative* in the *département* or, in advance, (state for which *département*) either from the French Government Tourist Office in London or by writing to the *Fédération Nationale des Gîtes Ruraux de France* (for addresses see pp.185-192).

The advantage of not booking in advance is that you can look at a *gîte*, or even several *gîtes* if there is a choice of more than one, before you decide to take one. However, if you want to play this game, it is essential that you give yourself enough time. Lets are from Saturday to Saturday (part of the week being payable as a complete week), and booking offices are closed on Saturday. You need to arrive at the booking office on Friday morning at the latest, making your inspections and be back at the booking office before it closes, probably at 5.30 p.m., to make a firm booking. Sometimes the addresses for available *gîtes* which you are given are at opposite ends of the *département*, and since some *départements* are surprisingly large and some of these small country places are not very accessible, you could find yourself spending a whole day just travelling back and forth between the booking centre and two *gîtes*. It is, therefore, essential to have detailed maps (yellow Michelin or *Institut Géographique National*, see list on pp.13 & 16) of the area, carefully pinpoint addresses when you are given them and seriously consider only those which are fairly close together and can be covered in one quick round-trip. With this method of booking you complete the rent contract and pay the total price for the rental at the *Relais Départemental*, who will inform the owner of your arrival by telephone.

Booking in Advance

For anyone used to have holiday arrangements neatly tied up before departure, it is advisable to book a *gîte* in advance, and for holidays in July and August it is essential. There are, basically, two ways in which this can be done:

1. Booking through the British Section of the Gîtes de France

To make use of this very convenient booking service you have to become a member of *Gîtes de France*, the current annual subscription (in 1983) being £2 (for London address see p.185). You will then be sent the current Official Handbook containing illustrated descriptions and prices of over 1,500 *gîtes* in all parts of France, including a number of *chambres d'hôte gîtes* (rural bed-and-breakfast accommodation), together with instructions on how to book. All the booking formalities are completed through the London booking office in English and there is no need to enter into correspondence with anybody in France, but the rent contract as such (an English translation of which is given in the Handbook), is with the owner of the chosen *gîte*. 30% of the rental, or in some cases the total rental, is payable by banker's draft in French francs before departure. In July and August any one *gîte* can be booked for a minimum stay of two weeks only, *chambre d'hôte gîtes* for 1 week, and for these two peak months the booking service advises its members to book early.

2. Booking directly with the owners or through a booking office in France

Theoretically, it is perfectly possible to write to a *Relais Départemental des Gîtes de France* or a *Loisir-Accueil* booking office (see p.187), ask for a list of *gîtes* in their *département* and take it from there: write to the owner, exchange contracts etc. etc. Or, if the booking office undertakes to make the booking for you, which is what the *Loisir-Accueil* offices do, let them complete the formalities. Unfortunately, these official *gîte* lists, although they list **all** *gîtes* for hire in a *département*, whereas the other publications mentioned in this book contain only a selection, are not usually illustrated and give only skeletal information, so that any choice you make is somewhat haphazard.

A better idea is probably to invest in the annual *French Farm and Village Holiday Guide* published by McCarta Ltd and available from bookshops early each year around £4.00. This carefully prepared book illustrates and describes a selection of about 1,000 *gîtes* in some 70 *départements*, including a number of chambres d'hôte (bed and breakfast). It gives detailed instructions on how to book (either directly with the owner or through a booking service), as well as sample booking letters in French and an English translation of the standard rent agreement. It also contains details of some Activity Holidays which can be booked through the *Loisir-Accueil* services.

What to take with you to a gîte

The most important item to take is bed and table linen. Exceptionally, an owner will furnish bed linen, and this will be stated in the description, but as a rule beds are equipped only with two blankets. It is a good idea to study the *gîte* description and bring the correct size of sheets for the beds provided. If you bring pillow cases you will probably have no use for them, because instead of a pillow as we know it the French traditionally use a long feather sausage called *traversin*. Unless you have a cover to fit this, which is unlikely, the only way to tackle it is to cover it with the bottom sheet.

We always bring sleeping bags and have often found them very useful in regions where the nights are cold and in *gîtes* where the blanket situation was unsatisfactory.

Towels, too, must be furnished by the tenant, and so must table linen. A tablecloth or place mats may not be essential, especially on a formica-covered table, but their presence does improve the look of the place. Tea-towels are never provided, and washing-up brushes and sponge cloths only rarely. There may be a gas-lighter for the cooker or there may not and it is advisable to take some matches.

To stand with wet feet on a bare bathroom or shower room floor is not everybody's idea of fun. Unless you want to use a towel for the purpose you would be well advised to bring a bath mat. Newspaper is no good, we have tried that: the print comes off on your feet!

There are not many food items that are better brought from home than bought in France. Instant coffee, which is expensive in France, and tea, or tea bags, are the only really obvious ones. If you, or your children, cannot do without such typically British things as Marmite, lime juice, baked beans or spaghetti in tomato sauce you should bring a stock of these. Small quantities of your favourite herbs and spices will be convenient to have, while a small jar of salt comes in handy to avoid having to buy a kilo bag of it. The same goes for French salad dressing, if you like your salads dressed. Unless you want to buy a large bottle of oil and vinegar each, most of which will not be used, you should make up a bottle of salad dressing at home and bring it with you. Detergent is not worth bringing. There is a liquid variety on sale in France now

(Vizir) which goes a long way and is very convenient to use on holiday.

Below is a **check list** of useful things to take with you:

Bed linen
Table linen
Hand and bath towels, bath mat
Tea towels
Sponge cloths
Washing up brush and pot scourer
Vim or liquid cleanser
Aluminium foil for cooking purposes
Plastic food bags
Matches
Elastic bands
Washing line and pegs
Iron and plug adaptor

Shopping note
If you begin your stay at a *gîte* on a Saturday afternoon, as is normal, do not forget to shop for everything you will need for Sunday and possibly Monday as well, before the shops close at 5.30 or 6 p.m. on Saturday. It is not safe to assume that there will be a food shop open on Sunday*, and many of the smaller ones are closed on Monday morning or all day Monday. Supermarkets and hypermarkets, on the other hand, usually open on Mondays.

Useful Phrases

Où est la boîte des fusibles?	Where is the fuse box?
Il n'y a pas de lumière	There is no light
Cette prise ne marche pas	This socket does not work
Cette ampoule ne fonctionne pas	This light bulb does not work
La cuisinière ne s'allume pas	The gas cooker won't light
La vieilleuse s'éteint	The pilot light blows out
La bouteille de gaz est vide	The gas cylinder is empty

*In very popular resorts, it is common to find a wide range of shops open on Sunday mornings.

Il y a une fuite de gaz	There is a gas leak
Il sent le gaz	There is a smell of gas
Comment fonctionne la chaudière (le chauffe d'eau)?	How does the boiler (the water heater) work?
Comment fonctionne la chauffage?	How does the heating work?
L'évier (le WC, le tuyeau) est bouché	The sink (the WC, the pipe) is blocked
Pouvez-vous le réparer?	Can you repair it?
Quand ramasse-t-on les ordures?	When is the rubbish collected?
Ou faut-il mettre la poubelle?	Where do I have to put the dustbin?

Furnished Apartments (*meublés*) other than gîtes

You may not wish to stay in a house in the depth of the French countryside but in a furnished apartment in a bustling lively town or resort. The Tourist Office of every town publishes, along with a hotel list, a list of private furnished apartments which are let during the season (see p.28). The definition of season may vary from place to place. For example, in a much frequented spa like Vichy season means all the year round. Current lists of *meublés saisonniers* are not usually available in this country. To get one you will have to write to the *Office de Tourisme/Syndicat d'Initiative* of the town in question. After having made your choice from the list, which gives basic details only, you write directly to the named proprietor who, if the apartment is free, will send you a detailed description, rent conditions, price, town plan with situation marker and possibly a photograph of the house. It is important, and required by law, to exchange a proper contract, signed by both parties. Once the contract is signed, the tenant, as with all other lets, is bound to pay the full rental price if he cancels the booking and the proprietor cannot otherwise let the apartment.

Unfortunately, the lists do not give prices. These are not fixed and are a matter of agreement between landlord and tenant. In practice it is probably not very advisable to hire a *meublé* ar arm's length unless you can obtain a photograph of it and already know the town so well that you are familiar with the situation of the apartment. A *meublé* is best hired on the spot. In July and August, when resort apartments are tremendously popular with French holiday makers, it is very difficult to find one free at short notice, but at any other time you can go to the *Office de Tourisme/Syndicat d'Initiative*, ask them to check what is free and go and look at it. With the recent setting-up of *Loisir-Accueil* booking offices (see p.10 and addresses p.187) it has become possible to hire some furnished houses and apartments, which are described and illustrated in their brochures, through them.

Villas

Flats and villas in many parts of France can also be hired through a great number of companies in the UK. Their names are listed in the annual Holiday Reference Guide published by the French Government Tourist Office in London (see p.10 and address list p.185). They can also be obtained from travel agents or found on the travel pages of national newspapers.

Camping and Caravanning

Some people prefer to take their camping or caravanning holiday as a single-site package deal inclusive of ferry crossing and overnight hotel stops, all booked and paid for in this country. There are many companies in the UK which offer this sort of holiday, which has the advantage that the tent or caravan is already waiting on a site in France. Names and addresses of some of these companies are published by the French Government Tourist Office in their Annual Holiday Reference Guide (see p.10). While this way of doing things is ideal for those who go camping only occasionally and do not want the permanent encumbrance of owning a tent or caravan, most committed campers like to take their own open-air home and make their own arrangements.

Camping is a very popular pastime in France. This is borne out by the liberal distribution of camp sites all over France, especially in popular holiday areas. Even tiny villages of 150 or so inhabitants have their municipal camp site, conspicuously signposted *camping municipal*. Municipal camp sites can be in any category, from one star to luxury, and some, despite their sober nomenclature, can be very good.

For detailed information of what campsites are where, how they are rated and what facilities they offer it is essential to buy at least one guide. Of the various publications on the market the annual *Michelin Camping Caravanning France* and the *Guide Officiel Camping Caravaning de la Fédération Française de Camping Caravaning* are probably the most comprehensive. Of these, if you are already using the red Michelin guide, the Michelin green guides and the yellow Michelin maps, the Michelin Camping Caravaning (obtainable from bookshops and motoring organisations in the UK) is the most useful, since its directions and maps tie in with the other Michelin publications. It lists about 3,500 sites of all categories which have been selected by Michelin's inspectors for their quality. Like all Michelin publications, it is clear and easy to use and employs self-explanatory symbols. It contains a list of sites where tents, caravans or bungalows can be hired.

The annual *Guide Officiel Camping Caravaning de la F.F.C.C.* on the other hand, lists *all* the equipped sites in France, including country camping and camping on farms (*campings à la ferme*), a total of over 8,500 sites. This guide, which is in French only, can be bought in the UK either from Hachette's French Bookshop, 4 Regent Place, London W1R 6BH. Tel. 01-734 5259 or by post, for £5.95 including postage and packing, from FFCC, 6 The Meadows, Worlington, Bury St. Edmonds, Suffolk, IP28 8SH.

All camping guides are having difficulty in ascertaining current prices charged on individual sites. For some sites prices are listed, for others they are not. The total price per day which one can be expected to pay is composed of the following separate items:

— fee per person (*redevance par personne*), abbreviated to *pers.*
— fee per car (*redevance par vehicule*), abbreviated to *veh.*
— fee for tent or caravan space (*redevance par emplacement*), abbreviated to *empl.*

The fee per person, which is generally half for children under 7, sometimes includes the free use of hot showers (*douche chaude*). On other sites showers are paid for by slot-meters. The fees for car and tent/caravan space are sometimes combined in one. Electricity supply is charged separately.

Based on 1983 prices the following is a rough guide to prices per day:

The fee per person can range from a minimum of 3F on a one-star site in a not-so-popular area without the use of hot showers to a maximum of 11F including hot showers and hot water in general, on a 4-star site in a very popular area.
The fee per car and tent/caravan space combined can range from a minimum of 3.50F to a maximum of 22F.
Electricity supply can cost between 2.50F and 8F.

You can work out for yourself that to stay on a campsite with a family of four can cost as little as 15.50F per day or as much as 74F per day. Some sites charge all-inclusive prices, so-called *forfaits*, which can be anything between 28F and 84F for two persons.

The most expensive sites are by the sea, on the Mediterranean and Atlantic coasts. They, too, are the most crowded, in July and August, to the point where camping becomes a doubtful pleasure. We would definitely recommend booking such a site in advance in the high season, by writing to the site operator at the address given in whichever guide you are using — not forgetting the postal code which follows the place name in the guide, but which should be written in front of it on the envelope. The site operator, when confirming, will ask for a deposit which will be deducted from the final bill.

That camping in the off-season is more enjoyable, because it is less crowded, than camping at the height of summer, is perhaps self-obvious, but for newcomers to camping one thing should, perhaps, be added: of the two low seasons, the early one is decidedly preferable. In May or June the grass is still green, the toilets and washroom still sparkling, the fittings still intact, and the warden still enthusiastic, but by October, when multitudes have trampled all over the site, everything will have taken on a well-used, worn and jaded look.

International Camping Carnet

An International Camping Carnet is not compulsory in France, but it is definitely advisable to have one. Some site operators actually refuse admission unless a carnet is shown.

A carnet can be obtained in the UK from the AA or RAC for a small fee and on completion of a form accompanied by a passport photograph, or, for members of camping/caravanning clubs, from their club.

The International Camping Carnet incorporates an indemnity on the part of the issuing body, i.e. a promise to pay, on your behalf, for any damage which you may cause to third-party property on a campsite which you visit. Alternatively, you may take out a separate third-party camping insurance with your insurance company. Whatever you do, remember to take the policy with you.

5. MOTORING

It is important to realise that France has over four times the area of the British Isles. Therefore, motoring distances are correspondingly large. Moreover, there are a number of outstanding physical features to be taken into account, the most important of which is the Massif Central, an ancient mountain block of volcanic origin rising in the centre of the country between the River Rhone in the east and bounded by a line Limoges — Toulouse in the west, and a line Poitiers — Moulins in the north and the Garonne Valley in the south. This natural barrier effectively breaks the southern half of the country into two, because travel across it is by no means easy. The roads are tortuous and difficult in all directions.

There are, too, the mountain regions of the Alps, stretching from *Lac Léman* (Lake Geneva) in the north to the Mediterranean in the south and only pierced by the occasional pass into Italy. However, several exciting routes can be taken in the north-south direction, bringing the motorist into very close contact with the mountains, especially at some very high mountain passes.

Then there are the Pyrenees, which separate France from Spain, again with very few passes, but with an exciting mountain road along its length.

The Jura and the Vosges are not so mountainous but still challenging to cross, and there is much hilly country in other parts of northern France, like most of Normandy, and much of the Brittany peninsula.

The final physical obstacle is Paris and its sprawling urban satellites and we have dealt with the special problem of getting past the capital on pp.61-63.

Bearing in mind the nature of the country, it is advisable to plan routes carefully, to be prepared to make detours for the sake of ease and speed, or simply to take the long way round rather than cut across difficult terrain. Of course, a lot of this difficult terrain provides the best scenery and the most interesting places to visit, so this factor, too, must be taken into account in any holiday motoring plans.

Finally, it is obvious that the size of the country, with a lower population than the UK, makes for a low density of traffic in rural areas so that motoring *can* still be what many people dream of, a serene frustration-free wander along traffic-free roads with time to enjoy the scenery.

French roads

The French are avid motorists. Whether this is the cause of their extensive road network or the result thereof is a matter for speculation. France is criss-crossed with a web of major and minor roads, and, on the whole, the surfaces are so good that even on narrow country lanes you can easily reach 80 km/h and still have a reasonably smooth ride. Exceptions are inevitable, and occasionally one finds that the road maintenance in one *département* is inferior to that in another, but on the whole one can confidently say that striking out into the depth of the French countryside entails no risk of broken shock-absorbers!

Since road surfaces are no problem, the main questions which have to be asked of the map before planning a route across country on minor roads are whether the route is straight, or hilly or winding and does it pass through many small towns. Villages are not usually a problem, but any small town which is at the intersection of a number of crossroads can cause considerable delay. If it happens to be market day when you arrive (often, but not always on Saturday), the problem will be magnified, since the roads invariably pass by or through the central square in which the market is held, and the local traffic can reach baffling proportions. Pedestrians do not consider that motorists are superior (indeed, why should they), so the roads are likely to be clogged with ambling shoppers who slow traffic down to a crawl. Of course, if time is no object, it is a bonus to come across a market day in a small town, but if you are pressed for time it is nothing but an irritation. When you do your advance planning, have a good look for the kind of town which may cause this problem. The map alone will not reveal all, you need to know how many inhabitants the place has. This is where the Guide Michelin comes in useful.

Our own experience as well as reports from friends and

acquaintances prove that cross-country travel on France's *routes départementales* (road numbers prefixed by the letter 'D') can be very brisk. If there are no major obstacles and the traffic is light, an average of 70 km/h is possible. Over long distances an average of 50-60 km/h is more likely, with the added advantage of low traffic density and the chance for the driver to see something of the countryside.

Minor roads can profitably be used to cut corners, eliminating dog-legs and, more importantly, to by-pass larger towns. There are times of the day when it is just as quick to go through the centre or along the periphery of a town, say between 10 a.m. and noon, between 1 p.m. and 2 p.m. and after 7 p.m. at night, but at all other times and especially before 9 a.m. or between 4 p.m. and 6 p.m. it pays handsomely to give larger towns a wide berth by branching off on to minor roads well before reaching the approach roads. Towns which stand at the crossroads of major north/south or east/west arteries, are particularly prone to traffic congestion. The evening rush, starting as early as 4 p.m., can bring everything to a virtual standstill, and this situation is made much worse by holiday traffic in July and August. The important thing is to leave the main road soon enough, say 10 km before the town periphery, and not to wait until the traffic in front of you slows down and you are trapped. We once sat in a traffic jam on the N7 just outside Moulins for one whole hour, between 4 and 5 o'clock in the afternoon, through having failed to leave this notoriously busy trunk road in good time. Eventually we saw an exit ahead which led to a *hypermarché* and when we eventually reached it we escaped gratefully and spent the next hour-and-a-half shopping and sitting in the cafeteria watching the traffic crawl past!

One of the joys of cross-country motoring is the discovery of the unexpected: idyllic spots by the river, long vistas across the countryside, small towns which you have never heard about but which prove little gems of interest and atmosphere. You can actually stop and look without holding up traffic or being troubled by the constant noise of passing cars and lorries.

One thing, though, cannot be stressed enough: do not be tempted to try to see too much in one journey, or in one day. In a country like France, which has so much to offer, this is all too easy. One is always driven to see just one more castle, one more ancient town before calling it a day.

The only way in which you can be reasonably sure of not overstretching your day is to start out with a modest mileage in mind and to allow time for planned (and un-planned) sight-seeing on the way. Sight-seeing en route is the commonest way of losing time. It literally slips away unnoticed. Even looking at one church or castle can cost up to two hours. A 'quick' walk round a town like Bourges or Rouen, which is bristling not only with ancient monuments but with exciting shopping streets, can cut over three hours out of your travelling day. On average, this kind of planned sightseeing will result in a mileage of about 120 miles a day, unless you make a start at the crack of dawn and/or use stretches of motorway in between. Even if you do only a modest amount of sightseeing, you will be pushed to exceed 200 miles in the day.

French Motorways (*autoroutes*)

There are now about 6,000 km (3,540 miles) of motorways in France, mostly converging on Paris and, in particular, connecting the north with the south and the east with the west. The centre of France, due to its mountainous character, has no east-west motorway connection, or at least not yet.

Tolls

With the exception of a few short distances, the motorways of France are subject to toll charges. One method is for a ticket to be issued to the motorist on entry to the toll section, most frequently by an automatic dispenser. You simply have to press the button marked with the symbol appropriate to your type of vehicle, whereupon a ticket is spit out. Be careful not to press the wrong button, e.g. that for a lorry, unless that is what you are driving, because the error cannot be corrected! The ticket is handed in at the exit point, where the appropriate toll is collected. You can work out what the charge should be from the information printed on the back of the ticket. On some short motorway sections the toll section is at the entry to the section: you simply throw the correct amount (which is displayed) into a basket, whereupon the barrier opens. If you need change, you have to select a lane in which an attendant is on duty.

The basis of toll charges is the distance travelled. However,

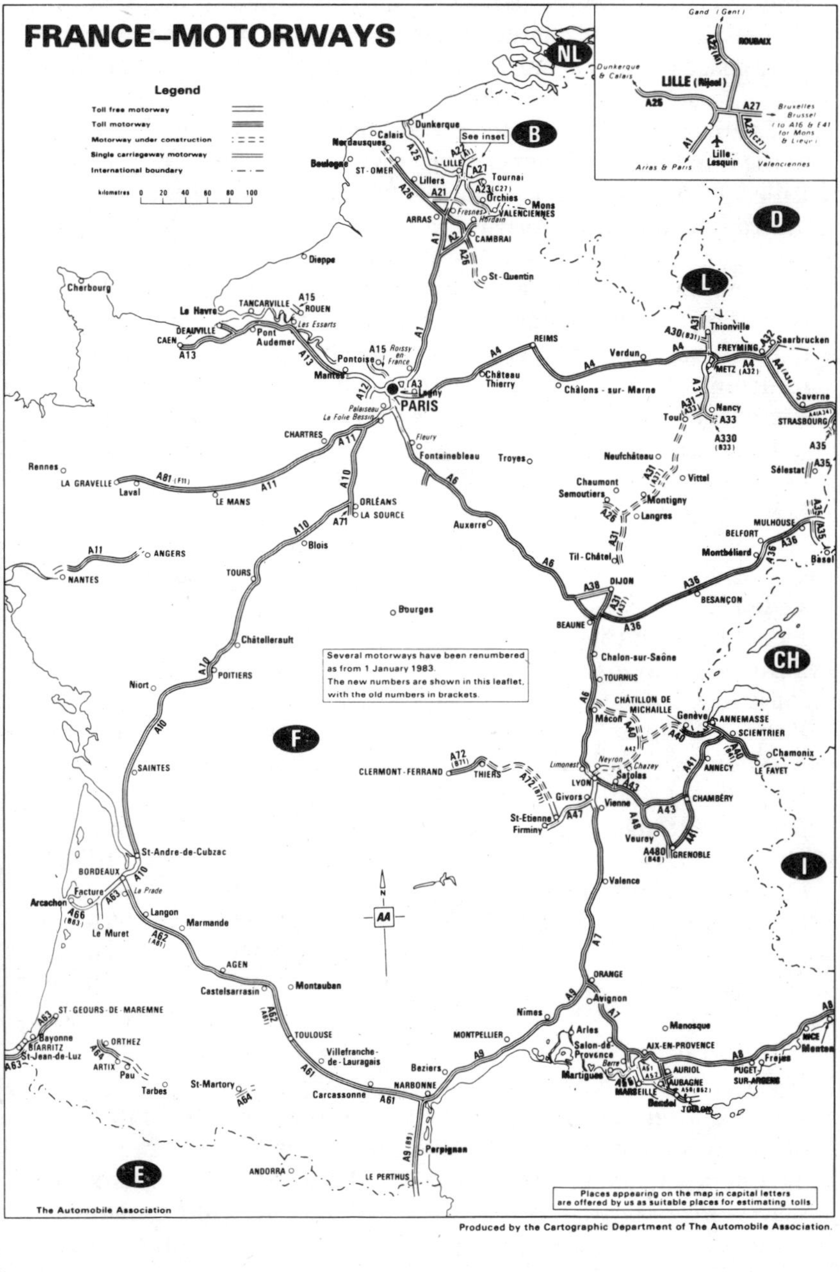
FRANCE–MOTORWAYS
Legend
Toll free motorway
Toll motorway
Motorway under construction
Single carriageway motorway
International boundary
kilometres 0 20 40 60 80 100
Several motorways have been renumbered as from 1 January 1983.
The new numbers are shown in this leaflet, with the old numbers in brackets.
Places appearing on the map in capital letters are offered by us as suitable places for estimating tolls.
The Automobile Association
NL
B
D
L
CH
F
I
E
See inset
Dunkerque
Calais
Nordausques
Boulogne
ST-OMER
Lillers
LILLE
Tournai
Orchies
Mons
VALENCIENNES
ARRAS
CAMBRAI
St-Quentin
Dieppe
Cherbourg
Le Havre
TANCARVILLE
ROUEN
DEAUVILLE
CAEN
Pont Audemer
Pontoise
Mantes
PARIS
REIMS
Château Thierry
Châlons-sur-Marne
Verdun
Thionville
METZ
Saarbrucken
Nancy
Toul
Saverne
STRASBOURG
CHARTRES
Fontainebleau
Troyes
Rennes
LA GRAVELLE
Laval
LE MANS
ORLÉANS
LA SOURCE
Auxerre
Blois
ANGERS
NANTES
TOURS
Bourges
DIJON
BEAUNE
BESANÇON
Montbéliard
MULHOUSE
BELFORT
Basel
Châtellerault
POITIERS
Niort
SAINTES
Chalon-sur-Saône
TOURNUS
Mâcon
Genève
ANNEMASSE
Chamonix
ANNECY
CLERMONT-FERRAND
THIERS
LYON
Givors
Vienne
St-Etienne
Firminy
CHAMBÉRY
GRENOBLE
Valence
St-André-de-Cubzac
BORDEAUX
Arcachon
Langon
Marmande
AGEN
Castelsarrasin
Montauban
ORANGE
Avignon
Nîmes
Arles
AIX-EN-PROVENCE
MARSEILLE
TOULON
Fréjus
NICE
Menton
MONTPELLIER
Beziers
NARBONNE
Carcassonne
TOULOUSE
Perpignan
LE PERTHUS
ANDORRA
Bayonne
BIARRITZ
St-Jean-de-Luz
ORTHEZ
Pau
Tarbes
St-Martory
ST-GEOURS-DE-MAREMNE
Gand (Gent)
ROUBAIX
Dunkerque & Calais
LILLE (Rijsel)
Bruxelles Brussel
Lille-Lesquin
Arras & Paris
Valenciennes

Produced by the Cartographic Department of The Automobile Association.

since different companies are involved in different motorways, there is no standard charge per kilometer. Clearly, some sections have cost a great deal more to construct than others, which is one of the reasons why the toll then is higher.

There are sections of motorway which are toll-free. These are in the immediate vicinity of large towns such as Paris, Bordeaux, Lille, Lyon, Marseille and Metz. Note that there are no indications on the motorways that these sections are free or how long they are. It is simply by experience that you acquire that information. Around Paris the toll-free sections are quite long, thus allowing free motoring within the urban area. It also means that a motorist can by-pass a large town by way of the motorway, returning to ordinary roads afterwards. Lyon is another good example of where this would be a useful thing to do.

Here are a few examples of tolls payable for some frequently used stretches of *autoroute*: They are to be used as a guide only, because tolls are subject to change.

	Car	*Car & Caravan*
Lilliers — Paris	36F	54F
Deauville — Paris	24.50F	35F
Paris — Le Mans	41F	61F
Paris — Bordeaux	130F	197.50F
Paris — Beaune	44F	68.50F
Mulhouse — Beaune	50F	75.50F
Beaune — Lyon	23F	35.50F
Lyon — Orange	37.50F	58F
Orange — Nice	62F	91.50F
Orange — Narbonne	41.50F	64.50F
Narbonne — Castelsarrasin	49.50F	77F
Narbonne — La Perthus	20F	31F
Bordeaux — Agen	29F	49F

Services

Petrol stations and toilets can be found on *autoroutes* at intervals of 20 to 40 km, which is quite an appreciable interval, and emergency telephones are installed about every 2 km. Parking places are indicated as *Aire de . . .* Some have filling stations, some are simply parking places with or without toilet facilities.

The most welcome ones, at least for children, are those on which a *frites* stand has been installed. These stalls are a common feature everywhere in France, in town centres as well as along busy road, and the chips they sell are really excellent. Snack bars can be found at not-too frequent intervals. *Count-Paille* (see p.135) have set up about 20 of their round, thatched-roof little grill restaurants on the exits of various motorway sections. There are also a number of more comprehensive drive-ins, like those under the *L'Arche* sign, which apart from reasonably-priced food and quick service offer rest rooms, washrooms, toilets and information. At the time of writing there is no official map of French autoroute facilities of the type which is published for German motorways, but there is an excellent motoring map showing the distribution of all *Courte-Paille* restaurants, *L'Arche* drive-ins, *Novotel*, *Sofitel*, *Mercure* and *Ibis* hotels, as well as Avis car hire centres, which can be obtained from Sofitel, 16 Berkeley Street, London W1X 5EA. Tel. 01-499 0734. It is entitled *La France du voyage*.

Petrol prices on French motorways, incidentally, vary but little from those generally prevalent, so that there is no point in leaving the motorway to fill up.

Traffic on motorways

Traffic on French motorways, in our experience, is lighter in general than on motorways in Germany, Belgium and Holland. There are noticeable fewer lorries, to start with, which is an indication of the lorry operators' unwillingness to pay the high tolls. You can expect, therefore, to find lorries on the major highways other than the motorways. Indeed, that is just what happens, and the major *routes nationales* (N-roads) can prove very difficult to drive at a good speed.

Despite the high cost we strongly recommend the use of the motorways for any long distance which has to be covered in a hurry and with the least strain on the driver, even when a small detour is involved to reach the nearest motorway or the overall mileage turns out longer.

Bypassing Paris

Giving Paris a wide berth will not necessarily make your life any easier. The best that can be said is that you will have a relatively pleasant run through the countryside, involving a fair amount of map reading and some quite hard driving, especially if you choose the western side. Assuming that Paris lies directly in your path it is far better to use the Paris ring road, the *boulevard peripherrique*. An occasional exception to this rule is when the BBC or French Radio specifically warns against doing so and recommends a by-pass.

On occasions the *boulevard périphérique* can get busy to the point of being totally choked. Since it is very wide, with up to six lanes and has innumerable entries and exits, it can become a real nightmare for someone just on his way through. You are only likely, though to meet these conditions in the very peak of the holiday rush, sometimes on a Sunday afternoon, when Parisians return home from a day out, and also at the peak traffic hours of the day when commuters are rushing to and from work. This includes either end of the lunchtime, at 12.00 noon and 2 p.m. Try to avoid the road at those times, but otherwise don't be put off. The exits are well sign-posted and, providing you have worked out in advance where you will have to leave it the *boulevard périphérique* holds no terrors. The red Michelin guide contains an excellent detailed map of the *boulevard périphérique*. While it would be pretty futile for the driver himself to try to refer to this while actually motoring, the co-driver, armed with the Michelin map, can easily follow progress and signal the appropriate exit. All exits are named after gates, i.e. *Porte*, (abbreviated *Pte.*), for example *Pte. de la Villette*, *Pte. de Pantin*, *Pte. de Lilas* etc., and as you follow the *boulevard périphérique* round so you eliminate them until you get to the one by which you want to leave (which you will, of course, have worked out in advance!). Exits to major destinations are also indicated on large signs, white on blue background, so that you can hardly go wrong. If you study the Paris map carefully before you reach Paris and acquaint yourself with the layout of the ring road, its exits, fly-overs and underground sections and also decide whether you want to follow it round clockwise or anti-clockwise, you will be able to negotiate it with equanimity.

The *Bison Futé* map, which is published annually by the French Ministry of Transport to assist holiday traffic and which is handed to motorists free on arrival at a French port (see also p.17), also has a very useful little map of the Paris ring-road and motorway layout. In years when major road works close sections on one or other of the two carriageways of the *boulevard péripherique*, *Bison Futé* indicates in which direction the boulevard must be negotiated. This invariably happens in July and August, when most Parisians have left for the country or the seaside and traffic round Paris is least dense.

When road works are particularly heavy, it is probably better to stay clear of it, at least during the day. The best time to use the ring-road, in any case, is at night, before 4 a.m., when traffic density is at its lowest and you have all the time in the world to sort out your route. The road is well lit and so are all the signs. Unless you want to visit the centre of Paris, do not try to cut across from one section of the *boulevard périphérique* to another. It is a recipe for disaster for anyone unfamiliar with the layout of the different sections of the city.

Motoring Topics

Documents required. A full licence is required; no L-plate driving in France. You also need the car registration papers, the insurance certificate, and an MOT certificate if the car is more than 3 years old, as well as a GB-plate on the back of the car. Minimum age for driving a car is 18, for a light motorcycle up to 80 cc it is 16.

Insurance. A Green Card, obtainable against payment of an additional premium from your insurance company, is no longer compulsory for visiting France, but it is definitely adviseable to have one. It gives you comprehensive cover when abroad, whereas without it your normal car insurance, even if it is fully comprehensive at home, will only cover you for the minimum Road Traffic requirements of the particular country, which is less than third party at home.

In addition to the Green Card, your insurance company should supply a European Accident Statement form. This statement, in duplicate, should be completed by both parties in the case of a motor accident, one copy each to be kept by both parties and submitted to their respective insurance company. It is not an admission of liability but a summary of identities and facts, which will speed up the settlement of claims. It is a tremendous help in recording all the right things in the heat of the moment.

If you are towing a caravan, a boat, a trailer or anything at all this must be covered separately by insurance.

Speed limits.

130 km/h (80 mph) on toll motorways
110km/h (68 mph) on dual carriageways, including toll-free motorways
90 km/h (55 mph) on all other open roads
60 km/h ((36 mph) in towns/built-up areas
90 km/h (55 mph) maximum speed in the first year after having passed the driving test
45 km/h (28 mph) if towing a caravan which exceeds 130% of the weight of the towing vehicle
75 km/h (45 mph) for light motorbikes between 51 cc and 80 cc

These speed limits are sometimes cancelled in special circumstances. Be careful to observe changes, since they invariably signal a traffic hazard. It is common to see a sign showing 60 km before an acute bend, simply because it is dangerous to negotiate it any faster. Police patrols often watch such points and catch offenders. Following a spate of accidents early in the holiday season, the intensity of police speed checks is invariably stepped up, and it is definitely not safe to be careless in this respect.

Note: for driving in wet conditions there are now special speed limits:

On toll motorways: 110 km/h
On all other roads: 80 km/h

Radar traps. Oncoming traffic flashing its headlights is almost certainly a warning of the presence of police ahead, and possibly of a radar speed trap.

Traffic Offences. Minor offences are dealt with by an on-the-spot fine. Speeding is dealt with severely (minimum fine 600 F) and so is non-observance of traffic signals and road markings. Two things in particular should not be gambled with: stopping at stop signs and not crossing solid white centre-lines. Driving when under the influence of alcohol falls into 2 categories: from 0.8 to 1.2 promille (proportion of alcohol in the blood) the offender, taken to a police station, is fined 120F on the spot. From 1.2 promille upwards it becomes a criminal offence which is punishable by very severe fines, even imprisonment, and the withdrawal of your licence for a period of from 6 to 12 months.

Seat belts. These must be worn by driver and front seat passengers. There is a fine for not doing so. The provision that children under 10 are not allowed in the front of a car which has a back seat is a very sensible rule.

Lights. Amber headlights are not compulsory for foreign tourists but they are definitely desirable. It is obligatory, however, to have headlights adjusted for right-hand driving, if only by affixing to the lenses one of the adhesive shapes available from car accessory shops and motoring organisations. Sidelights must never be used for driving, only for parking. If you have a car (e.g. Volvo) which has day driving lights as standard, take the fuse out unless you want to be constantly flashed and gesticulated at.

Full or dipped headlights should be used in poor visibility, and motor cycles must use dipped headlights at all times.

Compulsory spares/accessories. A complete spare bulb kit must be carried and should be bought *before* departure! Cars without flashing hazard warning lights must (and those with hazard warning lights should) carry a reflecting red warning triangle. In the case of an accident or break-down this must be set up in the road at a useful distance upstream.

Priority. The traditional 'priority from the right' rule is now largely replaced by the very much safer system by which one of the two intersecting roads has *passage protégée*, i.e. right of way. This is indicated by one of three signs:

Any road joining or intersecting a *passage protégée* road is marked with a stop or give way sign.

Priorité à droite (priority from the right) still operates in many built-up areas, though, and always in roundabouts. In built-up areas the only recipe against heart-failured caused by a car suddenly pulling out of a side-road immediately in front of you is to keep a close eye on traffic signs to make sure that you know when you do not have *passage protégée*, to be wary of side-roads on your right and to drive at a moderate speed. In roundabouts the flow is anti-clockwise and traffic from the right has priority, while traffic joining the roundabout has to give way. This takes a bit of getting used to and, among newcomers to the French traffic scene, is bound to result in a few shocks to the nervous system. The important thing is to keep your eyes open to the right once you are going round the roundabout!

Driving on the right: in practice this is easily adopted as the norm by drivers accustomed to driving on the left. Their only problems arise when wanting to overtake, as their visibility is restricted. This problem can be largely overcome by having a trustworthy person in the passenger seat to assist the driver with information on the current traffic situation ahead.

Traffic lights. Most traffic lights have small duplicate lights at eye-level which make it possible for the driver to pull up right alongside the traffic lights and still not lose sight of them. Lights change from red to green without the amber in between, and French drivers consequently tend to be slow in getting away from lights.

Parking. Large towns usually have extensive parking areas, either in the open or underground, and these are clearly indicated on town plans in the red Michelin guide. Parking fees are paid very much as in the UK: You get an adhesive ticket from a machine (which could cost, for example, 2F for an hour) and stick it inside the windscreen, or, in multi-storey car parks, you are given a ticket as you enter and pay as you leave.

Town centres usually have a *Zone bleue* where on-the-street parking is restricted (*stationnement réglementé*). Parking meters are common in such areas; they work exactly like ours. A typical charge would be 1F per half hour, with a maximum stay of 1 or 2 hours, but the charges do vary with the vicinity. If you see a sign that says *Zone bleue – Disque obligatoire* you do not have to pay to park there but you do have to display a clockface disc which, when rotated to show the time of arrival, will also indicate the required time of departure. The duration of the permitted stays varies according to the time of day, being shortest in the morning and afternoon shopping hours and longest in the lunchtime, from 11.30 onwards. These discs can be obtained for a few centimes, or even free of charge if they carry advertising, from petrol stations and *tabacs*. Any visitor can obtain one quite as easily as a resident.

Unilateral on-street parking is very common in France. This can be done in one of two ways. There is the *jours pairs/jours impairs* method by which cars have to be parked on one side of the road on even-numbered days (*jours pairs*) and on the other side on uneven-numbered days (*jours impairs*). This is very fair on residents on both sides of the road, but it does mean that car owners have to turn out at midnight to drive their cars across to the other side of the road. The alternative method is the one by which cars park on one side of the road from the 1st to the 15th of each month on on the other siude from the 16th to the 31st. If you see a red-and-blue non-parking sign with '1 — 15' written in it you know that you must not park on that side from the 1st to the 15th.

Free parking is often found in squares, in the vicinity of popular sights and meeting places such as churches, and under the trees planted on the sidewalks of boulevards.

When booking into a hotel it is important to remember that many of the older hotels in town centres do not have parking spaces. These hotels rely on visitors leaving their cars in roads nearby or in some convenient parking place not too far away. If you are forced into this position, do make sure that you take everything of value from the car even if you stay only for the night and even if the car is right outside the hotel and in full view of the night porter.

Filling stations. Petrol stations in large towns are invariably situated on the outskirts, on the roads in and out. Make sure you fill up before you have passed the last one, especially if you are about to make a cross-country journey. Filling stations in places remote from towns are sometimes few and far between and may have idiosynchratic opening hours. Within very small limits prices for different brands of petrol tend to be identical, but country prices are almost certainly higher than town prices. Some self-service garages do offer a substantial saving, and so do petrol pumps outside *hypermarchés*. Many petrol stations accept credit cards such as Access and Barclaycard/Visa. The French equivalent of Visa is called *Carte bleue* (blue card), and the familiar blue and yellow sign displayed in garage forecourts is defaced by the stylized letters 'cb'.

Car spares. More and more shops in France specialise in car spares, but the prices of spares for non-French cars are almost invariably higher, perhaps by as much as 30-50%, than one would pay in England. It is not a bad idea, therefore, to take along some essentials like fan belt, sparking plugs, contact breakers and, of course, a complete bulb kit, which you must legally carry. On the other hand, if your car is of French make, or you can find out which French model takes the same spares as your car, you can pick up some bargains in supermarkets.

Alternative routes (*itinéraires bis*). In the peak holiday period, when major through roads get congested, alternative, less busy roads are indicated by green or yellow panels or arrows. From 1982 onwards, to avoid confusion with the green road signs leading to large cities, which are gradually being introduced, more and more signs and arrows for alternative routes will be yellow and have *itinéraire bis* or *bis* actually written on them. Alternative routes are marked in the annual *Bison Futé* (see pp.17 and 62).

Towing a caravan. All the evidence is that holiday caravanning is on the increase throughout Europe. France, with its good road system and its many camping/caravanning sites is the ideal country not only for living in a caravan but for towing one. A few rules must be observed:

— Any vehicle towing a caravan must be equipped with an adequate rear view mirror (the police may test this at any time).
— The caravan's weight must not exceed that of the towing vehicle (including petrol, oil and water).
— The maximum permissible size of a caravan is 11 metres (long) × 2.5 metres (wide).
— A vehicle towing a caravan must remain at least 50 metres behind any vehicle ahead of it on trunk roads and motorways.
— Caravans must not travel in the outer left-hand lane of motorways.
— Caravans may not be towed in Paris.

Motorail. Motorail services, i.e. trains on which you can transport not only yourself but also your car, operate from Calais, Boulogne and Paris to destinations in all main holiday areas. This is a painless way of covering long distances north to south, especially if you make use of the sleeper facilities, but you don't see very much on the way, and it is expensive. The one-way fare, for example, for a car plus 2 adults from Calais to Nice, 2nd Class, including sleeper accommodation, was £225 (until May 1983). Anyone who abhors the long haul back at the end of a holiday could compromise and use it just for the return journey. Information can be obtained from French Railways, 179 Piccadilly, London W1V OBA, Major British Rail Travel Centres and from travel agents.

6. THE REGIONS OF FRANCE

Mainland France is divided into 21 tourist regions, which are, in fact, the country's regions for economic development.

Each region has its administrative headquarters for tourism — *Comité Régional de Tourisme* — based in the *préfecture* (principal town) of one of the departments of which the region is made up. In the details below this is indicated by an asterisk and the address

The Tourist Regions of France

will be found on p.186). In addition each department has a main tourist office in its *préfecture*.

Thus the 94 *départements* of mainland France are allocated to regions to which they broadly, from historic connections, belong. For ease of reference we have tabulated this information, together with a very short description of the main features of each region.

Alsace-Vosges-Lorraine

Départements	*Préfecture (with population)*	*Distance from Paris*
Meuse	Bar le Duc (20,500)	229 km
Moselle	Metz (117,200)	331 km
Meurthe-et-Moselle	Nancy (111,500)	306 km
Vosges	Epinal (42,800)	374 km
Bas Rhin	*Strasbourg (257,300)	488 km
Haut Rhin	Colmar (67,400)	444 km

This is a region of mountains and forests, with the important wine growing area of Alsace stretching from Marlenheim to Thann. There are many lakes, especially in the Vosges, and historic towns and villages like Strasbourg and Colmar, Metz and Nancy, Guebwiller and Riquewihr. There are several famous spas: Vittel, Contrexeville and Bains-les-Bains.

Aquitaine

Départements	*Préfecture (with population)*	*Distance from Paris*
Gironde	*Bordeaux (226,000)	560 km
Lot-et-Garonne	Agen (36,000)	641 km
Dordogne	Perigueux (37,600)	528 km
Landes	Mont de Marsan (32,000)	687 km
Pyrénées-Atlantiques	Pau (85,900)	750 km

Europe's biggest forest ($2\frac{1}{2}$ million acres) is in the Landes and there are over 280 kilometres of wide sandy beaches. The rivers Dordogne, Lot, Garonne, and Adour and the Pyrenees at the southern extremity all add up to make this one of France's most exciting regions. Settled in prehistoric times and by the Romans, the area has important historical connections.

Auvergne

Départements	*Préfecture (with population)*	*Distance from Paris*
Allier	Moulins (30,000)	293 km
Puy-de-Dôme	*Clermont-Ferrand (161,000)	400 km
Cantal	Aurillac (34,000)	545 km
Haute Loire	Le Buy (29,000)	516 km

Among the most popular of France's tourist regions, this is an area of forests, highlands and plateaux, river gorges and ancient volcanoes. The Cantal volcano crater was once 20 miles across. There are no less than 60 extinct volcanoes in the Puys de Dômes near Clermont-Ferrand, and they are only some 10,000 years old. The river valleys of the Allier and Loire are rich in castles and churches dating back many centuries. This is an exciting area, much of which is best explored on foot.

Brittany

Départements	*Préfecture (with population)*	*Distance from Paris*
Finistère	Quimper (60,500)	552 km
Côtes-du-Nord	St. Brieuc (56,300)	448 km
Morbihan	Vannes(43,500)	453 km
Ile-et-Vilaine	*Rennes (205,700)	344 km

The shores of Brittany make up one third of the total French coastline and have innumerable small harbours and much wild and romantic scenery. Inland there are miles of waterways and a countryside of hedgerows, orchards, fields of early vegetables and flowers. Attractive towns like Vitré with its medieval fortress, Dinant, St. Malo, Dinard, Vannes, Morlaix, Quimper beckon the tourist. This is a true holiday paradise.

Burgundy

Départements	*Préfecture (with population)*	*Distance from Paris*
Yonne	Auxerre (39,500)	167 km
Côte-d'Or	*Dijon (156,800)	312 km
Nièvre	Nevers (47,700)	239 km
Saônne-et-Loire	Macon (39,600)	395 km

With Greek and Roman origins going back to 600 *BC*, this is one of France's most historically rich regions. Since the 15th century its vineyards have produced some of the world's finest wines, with a cuisine to match. Châteaux, castles and churches are the architectural gems of the countryside. There are many interesting towns like Auxerre, Beaune, Tournus, Semur, Nevers, Sens and Dijon. Vézelay and Cluny are both outstanding examples of medieval religious architecture.

Champagne-Ardenne

Départements	*Préfecture (with population)*	*Distance from Paris*
Ardennes	Charleville-Mezieres (63,000)	225 km
Marne	*Chalons-sur-Marne (55,700)	188 km
Aube	Troyes (75,500)	158 km
Haute-Marne	Chaumont (30,000)	252 km

This is a landscape of vineyards, sunlit lakes and shady forests. There are no less than eight large lakes, the biggest being the Lac du Der-Chantecoq, which has an area of 12,300 acres. There is a famous wildfowl sanctuary in the Forêt d'Orient. The cathedral of Rheims is one of France's Gothic marvels, but there are many other architectural treasures including the Place Ducale at Charleville-Mezieres, half-timbered houses at Troyes and the fortified city of Langres with its massive ramparts.

Franche-Comté

Départements	*Préfecture (with population)*	*Distance from Paris*
Haute-Saône	Vesoul (20,000)	362 km
Doubs	*Besançon (126,000)	403 km
Jura	Lons le Saunier (23,000)	406 km
Territoire de Belfort	Belfort (57,000)	426 km

This region lies between the Swiss frontier and the River Saône. Here, the mountains of the Jura are green with forest and pasture, drained by innumerable swift-running streams. For those who enjoy a countryside of mountain passes and gorges, of rocky cliffs and wide plateaux, this is ideal. There are marvellous opportunities to explore the region on foot or on horseback.

Languedoc-Roussillon

Départements	*Préfecture (with population)*	*Distance from Paris*
Lozère	Mende (12,000)	572 km
Gard	Nîmes (134,00)	711 km
Hérault	*Montpellier (195,000)	760 km
Aude	Carcassonne (46,300)	905 km
Pyrénées Orientales	Perpignan (108,000)	908 km

This region has a great range of scenery, from the craggy, wild south of the Massif Central to the Pyrénées and the wide plains of the Mediterranean littoral round the Golf du Lion, where the largest volume of France's tables wine is produced. Vast sandy beaches fringe the Mediterranean, on which seven brand-new coastal resorts have sprung up in recent years including La Grande-Motte, Port-Leucate and Port-Barcarés. Roman remains abound, as do medieval castles and churches. Carcassonne remains Europe's largest existing fortified city.

Limousin

Départements	*Préfecture (with population)*	*Distance from Paris*
Creuse	Guéret (16,200)	352 km
Haute Vienne	*Limoges (147,000)	394 km
Corrèze	Tulle (21,600)	481 km

Limousin has hundreds of lakes and large areas of wild forest and heath-covered moorland. Castles, chateaux and churches blend into a gentle countryside in which lonely farmhouses and picturesque villages abound.

Loire Valley (centre)

Départements	*Préfecture (with population)*	*Distance from Paris*
Eure-et-Loire	Chartres (41,000)	88 km
Loiret	Orleans (110,000)	117 km
Loir-et-Cher	Blois (52,000)	181 km
Loir-et-Loire	*Tours (250,000)	234 km
Indre	Chateauxroux (60,000)	266 km
Cher	Bourges (80,000)	226 km

Rivers and vineyards and outstanding architecture, much of the time of the Renaissance, elevate this important middle section of the Loire to the front rank of France's most attractive tourist areas. Here are the greatest of France's châteaux, where French kings held court for centuries. Medieval Christianity, too, is remembered in the great cathedrals of Chartres and Bourges. Much fine food and wine make the region memorable, but above all this is France's land of castles: Chambord, Chenonceaux, Chevergny, Blois, Amboise and dozens of others.

Western Loire

Départements	*Préfecture (with population)*	*Distance from Paris*
Mayenne	Laval (55,000)	272 km
Sarthe	Le Mans (155,000)	203 km
Loire-Atlantique	*Nantes (263,000)	376 km
Maine-et-Loire	Angers (143,000)	288 km
Vendée	La Roche (48,000)	413 km

Over 300 kilometres of sandy beaches, with resorts as renowned as La Baule and Les Sables d'Olonne, make this a favourite area for those who enjoy the seaside. But there are more delights inland, with the wooded hills of Sarthe and Mayenne and the lower reaches of the Loire. There are fine castles like those at Angers, Nantes and La Lude and cathedrals at Le Mans and Luçon.

Midi-Pyrénées

Départements	*Préfecture (with population)*	*Distance from Paris*
Lot	Cahors (22,000)	593 km
Tarn-et-Garonne	Montaubin (50,400)	654 km
Aveyron	Rodez (28,200)	608 km
Tarn	Albi (49,500)	704 km
Gers	Auch (25,000)	712 km
Haute Garonne	*Toulouse (383,200)	705 km
Ariège	Foix (10,200)	788 km
Haute Pyrenees	Tarbes (57,800)	770 km

This is France's largest single region with some of the greatest contrasts, from the high mountains of the Pyrénées to the plains of the Garonne valley, the Gorges du Tarn and the Causses. Here is wild beauty in the countryside, while little towns bristle with towers, and castles cling to sheer rock faces.

Normandy

Départements	*Préfecture (with population)*	*Distance from Paris*
Manche	Saint Lo (25,000)	303 km
Calvados	Caen (123,000)	240 km
Orne	Alençon (35,700)	194 km
Eure	*Evreux (50,400)	102 km
Seine-Maritime	Rouen (118,300)	139 km

Here is some of France's finest farming country with golden cornfields, rich pastures and limpid rivers. Prosperous, with a distinctive architecture. Normany produces the world famous Camembert cheese and fine cider, to say nothing of *Calvados*, the world-renowned fiery apple brandy of the region. Sandy beaches stretch for many miles along the western reaches of the coast. Famous cathedrals are found at Bayeux, Rouen and Coutances, Sées and Evreux, while Mont-St. Michel is a marvel without parallel.

Nord-Pas de Calais

Départements	*Préfecture (with population)*	*Distance from Paris*
Pas de Calais	Arras (50,300)	178 km
Nord	*Lille (177,000)	219 km

The region has a coastline (the Opal coast) with over 128 kilometres of sandy beaches, cliffs and dunes, contrasting with an undulating hinterland, which merges in the plain of Flanders in the north. Here, too, there are immense forests. The towns have considerable historic importance, and there are many old fortresses to bear witness to a history in which frontier wars have played an important role.

Paris (Île de France)

Départements	*Préfecture (with population)*	*Distance from Paris*
Yvelines	Versailles (97,000)	22 km
Seine	*Paris (9,000,000)	
Seine-et-Marne	Melun (39,800)	56 km

Paris is the heart of France and was once surrounded by forests. Some of those remaining are near the famous châteaux of Versailles, Fontainbleau, Dampierre, Ramouillet and St. Germain. Paris itself is a treasure-house of interest, with sufficient to keep the traveller entertained for many visits.

Picardy

Départements	*Préfecture (with population)*	*Distance from Paris*
Somme	*Amiens (136,000)	149 km
Oise	Beavais (56,700)	76 km
Aisne	Laon (30,000)	135 km

This is a rural area with enormous, wide-ranging fields, and undulating farmland interspersed with woods and intersected by streams and rivers. There are also great forests like those of Chantilly, Compeigne, Retz, Crecy and Coucy. The region has many historic sites with great Gothic cathedrals at Amiens, Beauvais and Laon, as well as castles and chateaux.

Poitou-Charente

Départements	*Préfecture (with population)*	*Distance from Paris*
Charente	Angoulême (50,000)	443 km
Charente Maritime	La Rochelle (81,900)	471 km
Deux Sèvres	Niort (70,000)	408 km
Vienne	*Poitiers (28,700)	333 km

This regions has over 250 miles of coastline with a good many sandy beaches. In the south are Royan and the Côte de Beauté. Inland there is a peaceful countryside, much of it devoted to wine growing and the production of cognac, as well as excellent farm produce.

Provence

Départements	*Préfecture (with population)*	*Distance from Paris*
Vaucluse	Avignon (92,000)	687 km
Bouches-du-Rĥone	*Marseille (914,000)	777 km
Hautes Alpes	Gap (29,000)	667 km
Alpes de Hte. Provence	Digne (16,000)	744 km
Var	Draguignan (25,000)	863 km

Provence, with its outstanding climate and striking natural beauty, was so named by the Romans as the *province*, since it was nearest to Italy and so most like home. It is the richest of France's regions in Roman remains, but has many other outstanding historic towns, not least among them Avignon. There are several nature parks including Les Ecrins and the Camargue.

Rhône-Loire

Départements	*Préfecture (with population)*	*Distance from Paris*
Ain	Bourg en Bresse (45,000)	426 km

Rhône	*Lyon (462,000)	462 km
Loire	St. Etienne (221,000)	521 km
Ardèche	Privas (11,200)	602 km
Drôme	Valence (70,300)	561 km

Here is the highway to the sun, taking the traveller from north to south down the Rhône valley. The contrasts in scenery are outstanding: from the hills and lakes of the southern Jura to the vineyards of the sunny Drôme and Southern Alps. The Massif Central starts in the rocky outcrops of the Ardèche, while at its heart lies the gastronomic and commercial centre of Lyon.

Riviera (Côte d'Azur)

Départements	*Préfecture (with population)*	*Distance from Paris*
Alpes Maritimes	*Nice (346,000)	933 km

The sea is always blue and the pine-clad hills extend nearly to the sea against a background of snow-capped Alps. This is the region of France which the English and others made popular as early as the 18th century. Its summer crowds only reflect the great attractions of this sunny coast with its many outstanding holiday resorts.

Savoy and Dauphiny

Départements	*Préfecture (with population)*	*Distance from Paris*
Haute Savoie	Annecy (55,000)	548 km
Savoie	*Chambéry (56,800)	560 km
Isère	*Grenoble (169,700)	568 km

Here are the largest lakes and the tallest mountains in France, and including the nature parks of La Vanoise, Les Ecrins and Vercors this region is a paradise for the walker and climber, and all those who enjoy the great outdoors. There is also a first class choice of accommodation and recreation. Annecy is one of France's most pleasant towns, ideally situated on a large lake.

7. REGIONAL FOOD SPECIALITIES

Gastronomically speaking France cannot be divided into the regions by which it is organised by the national tourist authority. This would be too simple and arbitrary a way of tackling the subject. It is therefore necessary to look for traditional subdivisions of the country, in which the natural products are related to the cuisine. The result is a somewhat less well-defined breakdown, with the so-called regions rather blurred at the edges where they overlap. Over the years of seeking a suitable reference for this culinary regionalisation we have constantly been drawn back to that outstanding French work of reference, *Larousse Gastronomique.** It is on the sub-division of the country as recommended in this book which we have based this short survey.

The gastronomy of France is far too large a subject to be dealt with in any detail in a book of this nature. However, a selection of what is peculiar to each region will at least give an idea of what to look for when studying restaurant menus or shopping in search of local specialities.

One cannot be categorical, however, about saying that anything is exclusive to any one region; the fame of many regional dishes and products has spread not only throughout France but worldwide, to the point where many dishes can be found on the menus of imaginative restauranteurs everywhere; and food products which were once local, such as *Rillettes de Mans*, are now found in shops the length and breadth of the country. It is, nevertheless, interesting to know the traditional origin of a dish, though even here one must add the proviso that many dishes may have had more than one place of origin since their ingredients have been produced in many parts of the country from time immemorial.

---

*Larousse Gastronomique is published in the UK by the Hamlyn Publishing Group.

The Food Regions of France

Artois, Boulonnais and Picardy

This region is often ignored by tourists passing through from the Channel ports on their way to more interesting places. The area is, however, of gastronomic interest and has much fine food.

Boulogne, France's main fishing port, enjoys outstanding seafood, and all the beef, poultry and game found in the region are good. There are excellent vegetables.

Specialities

Charcuterie especially *andouilles*, *saussice de campagne*, black puddings and smoked ham
Cider and beer, which often appears in soup in Artois
Shellfish, especially mussels and cockles and lobsters
Herrings (now in shorter supply) and mackerel, especially in Boulogne
Pâtisserie at Boulogne, the finest in the region (some say in France)
Cheese *Marolles*, a soft, fairly strong cheese similar to Pont L'Evêque

Some dishes

Hochepot a fatty broth of pig's ears and tails, pieces of beef, mutton and all kinds of vegetables; a dish said to be rarely found these days
Moules marinières mussels cooked in white wine with shallots and herbs
Coquilles Saint-Jacques scallops, either deep-fried or served in their shells in a sauce and browned on top
Flamiche leek flan
Pâté de canard d'Amiens duck pâté from Amiens
Tarte de pommes apple tart
Lapin de Garenne wild rabbit with prunes

Champagne/Ardennes

The fame of this area rests on the production of its great sparkling wines. Gastronomically, the region is not thought to match the excellence of some others, though there are many dishes which will excite the palate. The local *charcuterie* is first class and there are fine fish from freshwater sources.

Specialities

Candied and sugared almonds from Verdun
Smoked ham

Pig's trotters
Turkeys — the region is a great breeding centre
Snails
Andouillettes de mouton, sausages made from lamb
Charcuterie, especially from the environs of Chaumont
Cheese: *Carré de l'Est* a square cheese made from cow's milk, tasty and long-lasting

Some dishes
Potée Champenoise a thick soup of pork and vegetables
Quartier de mouton à la champagne shoulder of mutton cooked with champagne
Boudin de lapin a sausage made with the meat and blood of rabbit
Matelots fish stews made with champagne
Escargots snails of the *petit-gris* variety, prepared according to various methods
Beignets de fromage blanc fritters made with cottage cheese

Lorraine

Lorraine has a fine cuisine, though there is a tendency for the dishes to be rather substantial. Outstanding *charcuterie* stands alongside the products of poultry and cattle raising, and the freshwater fish in the rivers provide excellent ingredients. It is a point of honour to eat well in Lorraine, an area of large towns and heavy industry, as well as fine countryside.

Some specialities
Beer from Metz and Nancy, both light and dark
Fruit brandies: quetsch, mirabelle, raspberry, cherry, pears
Quiches with a variety of fillings
Pastries and cakes of all kinds
Charcuterie

Some dishes
Quiche Lorraine a tart made of eggs, bacon and cream
Tourte à la Lorraine a tart of veal and pork
Tourte aux oignons onion tart
Boudin de Nancy black pudding from Nancy

Terrine de canard duck pâté
Potée de lard a thick soup with bacon
Cuisses de grenouilles au gratin frog legs *au gratin*
Quennelles de foie de veau calf's liver dumplings
Madeleines de Commercy small sponge cakes
Macarons de Nancy

Alsace

Strasbourg has long been famous for its *charcuterie* and for the famous *pâté de foie gras* of the region. The whole area is one of good food and wines, with pork, goose, vegetables and freshwater fish top of the list of ingredients

Some specialities

Saucisses de Strasbourg which resemble Frankfurters, but are redder in colour and sold all over France, usually pre-packed
Charcuterie, like black puddings with tongue, liver sausage, veal roll and saveloys
Pâté de foie gras goose liver pâté with truffles (the most famous comes from Limersheim and Hildersheim)
Jambon fumée smoked ham
Cheese: the most famous is *Munster Gerome*, a powerful, semi-hard cheese from the town of Munster, nr. Strasbourg, rather like a *Pont l'Evêque*
Honey, especially *Miel de Sapin*, which comes from the tips of the needles of silver fir trees
Pastry, especially *kugelhupfs* (round cakes with a hole in the middle) and *bretzels* and *beignets* (fritters)
Fruits in syrup and jams, especially mirabelles and quetsch plums, cherries, bilberries, and raspberries.

Some dishes

Choucroute garni sauerkraut with sausages, ham and fat bacon
Rôti de porc avec quetsches roast pork with quetsch plums
Cuisses de grenouilles frog's legs, sautéed with garlic butter
Paupiettes de veau veal olives
Salmi d'oie casserole of goose meat
Crèpes au kirsch pancakes with cherry liqueur

Brittany

A great choice of food products makes this region important gastronomically in France. The poultry, beef, pork and mutton are all of the highest quality, and Breton butter has long been considered to be as good as that of Normandy. The long coastline naturally provides the ingredients for an enormous variety of seafood dishes. The area is also known for its fine early vegetables, many of which are exported, but the majority of which find their way to the Paris market and other parts of France.

Some specialities
Cider and apple juice
Oysters from the Belon River and all manner of crustaceans
Chickens, the esteemed *poulet blanc Breton*
Ham from Morlaix
Pancakes and girdle cakes made from buckwheat; *brioches*
Rillettes, pâtés de campagne, andouilles (chitterling sausages)
Ducklings, especially from Nantes

Some dishes
Coquilles Saint-Jacques scallops, deep fried or in a sauce au gratin
Brochet au beurre blanc pike in a sauce made with butter and shallots
Gigot d'agneau roti à la bretonne roast leg of lamb with beans
Boudins noirs black puddings
Cotriade Breton fish soup
Caneton braisé Nantes duckling braised

Normandy

This region of France has one of the highest reputations for gastronomic excellence, which is based, not least, on the superb quality of its farm produce. Of special importance in the Normandy cuisine are butter and cream, which give many of the dishes their rich, luxurious flavour.

Specialities

Oysters from Saint Vaast and La Hougue, mussels and many other shellfish, including lobsters and crabs
Sole, mackerel, herrings
Poultry
Mutton from the salt meadows of the Cotentin Peninsula
Butter, especially from Isigny
Cheeses: *Camembert*, *Pont l'Evêque*, *Boursin*, *Livarot*, *Gournay*, *Neufchâtel*
Cider, which is semi-sweet and very smooth
Calvados (apple brandy) and *Bénédictine* liqueur from Fécamp

Some dishes

Sole Normande sole cooked in white wine and served in a cream sauce
Langouste à la creme lobster in cream sauce
Marmite Dieppoise stew of fish and vegetables
Tripes à la mode de Caen tripe cooked with cider and *calvados*
Poulet vallé d'Auge chicken in cream sauce
Poulet farci stuffed chicken
Coq au Chambertin capon in red wine
Caneton à la Rouennaise roast duck stuffed with forcemeat and served with red wine sauce
Jambon au cidre ham cooked in cider
Oeufs à la creme eggs cooked on croutons and covered with a rich cream sauce
Omelette à la Normande this can either be an omelette filled with shrimp's tails and mushrooms, or an apple omelette *flambée* with calvados
Soupe à cresson watercress soup
Mirlitons de Rouen flaky-pastry tartlets filled with a kind of vanilla-and-orange flavoured custard
Tarte aux pommes apple tart

Ile de France

Paris is the centre of the Ile de France and its gastronomy benefits from a wide range of imported foods as well as all the excellent products of the surrounding countryside. First-class vegetables and fruit can be found, while the meat sold in the Paris butchers is among the best in France. Even game is to be had from the forests around Versailles, Marley and St-Germain-au-Laye.

Specialities

Asparagus from Laôn; and also artichokes
Champignons de Paris
Veal and sweetbreads
Charcuterie of the highest order
Cheeses: *Brie* and *Coulommiers*. (According to the Duke of Talleyrand, Napoleon's Foreign Minister and a great gastronome, Brie was the King of Cheeses). *Mimolette*, which resembles *Edam*, but is harder and more tangy in flavour
Mustard from Meaux
Bread, especially the Parisian *baguette*
All manner of pastries and cakes: *choux à la crème (cream puffs)*, *éclairs au chocolat*, *St Honorés* (cream puffs with whipped cream) etc.
Outstanding confectionery, like chocolate truffles

Some dishes

Sauté de veau Marengo a kind of *ragoût* of veal in white wine, reputedly invented by Napoleon's chef after the battle of Marengo. The same recipe is used with chicken
Langouste à la creme lobster in cream sauce
Noix de veau braisé filet of braised veal
Poulet chasseur chicken garnished with mushrooms, shallots and moistened with white wine
Boeuf à la mode beef marinaded in red wine, cooked with onions and carrots
Jambon à la maillot ham braised in Madeira wine

Anjou

Anjou cattle and pork are greatly prized. The dairy products of the region have a reputation closely approaching those of Normandy, and certainly the butter is in no way inferior. Chicken, fish from the rivers, especially pike and tench and bream, and above all, the Loire salmon are all most highly regarded. Superb fruit comes from the orchards of this sunny province; pears, apples, plums and strawberries to name a few.

Specialities
Rillettes d'oie rillettes of goose, also of chicken
Cremets soft fresh cream cheeses eaten with sugar
Cointreau liqueurs from Angers
Beurre blanc White creamy butter
All manner of charcuterie, white puddings and black puddings.

Some dishes
Poulet du Mans chicken le Mans style
Capon à la flêche capon roasted on a spit over a charcoal grill
Brochet au beurre blanc the famous butter of the region
Matelote d'anguille eel stew with red wine
Alose farci shad stuffed with breadcrumbs, butter, onions, parsley and chervil
Poulet fricassé chicken in white sauce
Bijane a cold soup made by putting crumbled bread into sweet red wine

Orleanais

Like so many other regions of France, the Orleanais has all the prerequisites of a gastronomic region of repute: fine cattle and sheep, plentiful game, excellent poultry, fish from the river Loire and high-quality fruits and vegetables from the orchards and market gardens of the sunny Loire valley.

Specialities
Game pâtés
Rillons and *rillettes* notably from Le Mans, Blois and Vendôme
Carp, pike and salmon
Asparagus
White vinegar from Orléans
Cider
Beaugency fruit pâté

Some dishes
Matelote fish stew
Brochet à la marinière pike in white-wine sauce
Carpe à la Chambord braised, stuffed carp, beautifully garnished
Mauviettes en timbale or *en croute* larks in a pie crust
Gâteau de Pithiviers puff pastry with a filling of rum-flavoured almond paste
Terrine de lièvre potted hare
Pâté de lapereau wild rabbit pâté

Touraine

There is an abundance of every kind of food for the table in this prolific region, the home of the French writer Rabelais, who created Gargantua, a huge giant with a vast capacity for food and drink. There are fish from the rivers, butter, veal, pork, vegetables and fruit of all kinds. *Charcuterie* from Touraine is renowned.

Specialities
Rillettes and *rillons* (see section on charcuterie, p.000)
Andouilles and *andouillettes* (see section on charcuterie, p.000)
Fish, especially pike and carp
Apples, pears and other summer fruit
Cheeses: *St. Paulin* (yellow, mild and creamy), *Valencay*, *St. Maure* and *Selles-sur-Cher* (all goat's milk cheeses)
Stuffed prunes and dried prunes
Mushrooms

Some dishes
Matelote d'anguille eel stew
Filets de Sole à l'américaine sole in white sauce
Fricassée de poulet chicken in white sauce
Champignons farcis stuffed mushrooms
Noisette de pork aux pruneaux fillet of pork with prunes and cream sauce

Berry

The cuisine of the region of Berry, with Bourges as its capital, is characterised by simplicity. Indeed many of the dishes are quite peasant in nature and origin, though they are produced from a well-stocked larder. Sheep raising is famous, there is fine poultry from Bourges itself and a great deal of fish and game from the surrounding rivers and woods.

Specialities
Poultry and game
Confectionery, like gingerbread, biscuits, petit fours, cherry flans (*clafoutis*), and marzipan cakes
Lamb and mutton
Trout, carp, crayfish and lampreys
Goats milk cheeses

Some dishes
Coq au vin chicken in red wine sauce
Soupe grasse aux truches thick potato soup with salt pork
Citrouillat pumpkin pie
Grignaudes flat country cakes made with pork crackling
Poulet en daube casserole of chicken
Amourettes de veau à la crème veal marrow in a cream sauce

Burgundy

Not only is Burgundy famous for its splendid wines, but it has a very high gastronomic reputation as well. Dijon was, in fact, the scene of the very first gastronomic fair to be organised in France.

Specialities
Snails (*escargots*) large succulent, mainly from the vineyards and cooked *à la Bourgignonne* (with garlic butter)
Crayfish
Mustard from Dijon, as well as many pickles
Hams from the Morvan country, smoked ham of top quality
Charolais cattle, which provide the finest beef
Jams from Bar-le-Duc and Gevrey-Chambertin

Aniseed balls from Flavigny
Candied fruits
Crème de Cassis blackcurrent liqueur made with brandy. This is mixed with white wine to make the famous local aperitif, *Kir*

Some dishes
Boeuf à la bourguignonne (or simply *bouef bourguinon*) braised beef in a red wine, onion and mushroom sauce
Poulet à la creme
Brochet à la creme
Ecrevisses à la creme
Jambon à la creme
} Chicken, pike, crayfish, ham resp. in cream sauce
Grenadins de veau pieces of thick topside of veal studded with bacon fat
Rigodon a delicious baked pudding with lots of eggs, chopped hazelnuts and walnuts in it, served with fruit purée poured over. Can also be made as a savoury entrée with ham in it
Rable de lièvre saddle of hare
Meurette freshwater fish stew
Pâté de gibier game pâté
Quenelles de brochet pike dumplings
Nonnettes de Dijon iced gingerbread cakes

Franche-Comté

This mountainous region along the Swiss frontier is rich in all manner of edible products. The beef and milk cattle are famous; the high quality milk produces cheese of outstanding fame. There is a great deal of game, while the rivers, as always in France, teem with fish of all kinds.

Specialities
Cheeses: Comté (a form of *Gruyère*), *Septmoncel* (similar to *Roquefort*) and *Fromage fort*
Butter
Chocolate
Sausages and smoked ham
Kirsch a spirit distilled from wild cherries
Pastilles des Vosges (sweets made from the resin of fir trees)

Some dishes
Barquettes (savoury tartlets in the shape of a boat)
Quennelles de brochet pike dumplings
Tourte à l'oignon onion tart
Poulet farci à la cervelle chicken stuffed with brains
Potage de cuisses de grenouilles frog's legs soup
Omelette au kirsch

Poitou

All manner of poultry is raised, while the coastal regions produce excellent fish and shellfish. The fertile countryside produces a wide range of vegetables and there is good mutton, pork and beef.

Specialities
Oysters, mussels and lobsters
Rabbits, hares and duck
Crayfish
Onions, cauliflowers and green cabbages
Eels and frogs from the coastal marshes

Some dishes
Potée à la tête de porc pig's head soup
Matelote a'anguille eel in red wine
Pâté de Paques Easter pie, filled with minced meat, eggs and pieces of pork and chicken
Chouée green cabbage with butter
Chaudrée fish stew
Lièvre à la vendéenne hare cooked in the local style

Angoumois

With excellent food products, this region can hardly avoid having a high gastronomic reputation. Game and fish of all kinds are found everywhere, especially trout, eels and crayfish. Mushrooms of all kinds are found wild, but large quantities are cultivated in the quarries near Angoulême. Good beef cattle are reared, while the Barbezieux chickens have a high reputation.

Specialities
Snails
Mushrooms
Oysters, clams, mussels and a whole range of other shellfish
Chickens and capons
Partridges and hares
Trout, crayfish and eels

Some dishes
Tourtière raised chicken pie
Cagouilles farcis stuffed snails of the local variety
Friture charentaise small local fish of all kinds fried together
Pâté de foie gras truffée truffled liver pâté made from the livers of a variety of animals
Confit de canard preserved duck eaten with potatoes fried in goose fat
Fouaces hearth cakes
Farée stuffed cabbage

Guyenne

This very large area is famous for its wines, but it is equally well-known for its cuisine, which is extensive and imaginative. Garlic and truffles (from Périgord and Lot) are extensively used for flavouring. A great deal of fruit and early vegetables are grown in the region, while fish from the rivers, a wide range of game from the woods and vineyards, as well as geese and ducks raised for the market, provide excellent ingredients.

Specialities
Peaches and early vegetables from Montauban
Truffles from Périgord, used in the famous foie-gras and a great variety of other dishes
Prunes from Agen also prepared in Armagnac
Marrons glacés candied chestnuts
Confit d'oie potted goose
Walnuts and walnut liqueur
Jams and preserves of all kinds from the wide variety of fruits

Some dishes

Entrecôte bordelaise entrecôte steak in a red or white wine sauce with marrow bone fat

Fricassée d'anguille persillée eel in white sauce with parsley

Foie de veau bordelaise calf's liver in red wine sauce

Cèpes à la bordelaise boletus mushrooms in a wine sauce

Oie farcie avec pruneaux goose stuffed with prunes

Garbure a broth made with pickled goose and various herbs

Pâtes de grives thrush pâté

Filet de boeuf braised in a stock with slivers of truffles inserted in the meat *à la périgourdine*

Marche and Limousin

Limoges, at the centre of this region is among the great gastronomic centres of France. The area is famous for its pigs and cattle, game, poultry and freshwater fish, especially carp, trout, pike and crayfish. Walnuts and chestnuts and all kinds of fruit grow well, while the woods are rich in edible fungi.

Specialities

Foie gras et truffé this is duck or goose liver pâté with truffles, which have been sniffed out from under the trees by trained pigs

Brou, Ratafia, Eau-de-noix liqueurs made from walnuts

Confit d'oie the much-prized conserve of goose pieces in their own fat, which are served with fried potatoes

Marrons glacé candied chestnuts, which are world famous

Jams and jellies, made from the various fruits of the region — peach, quince, cherry, figs, pears, strawberries, plums and greengages

Some dishes

Lièvre à la royale hare stuffed with its own intestines, foie gras and pork fat. This is a great speciality dish of this region

Canard à la Limousine duck with red cabbage

Cèpes farcis stuffed mushrooms (boletus)

Boudin avec marrons black pudding with chestnuts

Ballotines de dinde et perdreau terrines of turkey and partridge

Soupe au choux cabbage soup
Clafoutis cherry tart

Auvergne

Good vegetables and fruit are grown in this region; its chestnuts and walnuts are well known. Mutton is particularly good, and very fine cattle is reared in the mountain pastures. The pork, as in many parts of France, is excellent. The woodlands are rich in game, as are the rivers, ponds and streams in fish, especially carp, pike, eels and trout and crayfish.

Specialities
Hams from Ussel, Aurillac and Saint Mathieu
Salmon from the Allier, trout and crayfish
Salaison salted meats and meat products
Poultry (though not as good as that of Bresse)
Cèpes (boletus mushrooms much prized all over France)
Crystallized fruit from Clermont-Ferrand
Mineral waters, especially from Vichy
Cheeses: *St. Nectaire* (creamy with a delicate taste)
Cantal (vague resemblance to Cheddar)
Bleu d'Auvergne (veined, with a sharp, fresh flavour)
Fourme d'Ambert (a blue cheese, made for over 2,000 years)
Caperon (a farmhouse cheese flavoured with garlic)

Some dishes
Oie farci stuffed goose
Fricandeaux small pork pâtés cooked in a caul wrapper
Tripaux sheep's trotters and veal offal stuffed with seasoning
Salmis de mouton a kind of lamb casserole made with pre-roast lamb
Truffade fried potatoes with bacon, garlic and cheese
Tourte de viande and *tourte à la volaille* meat and chicken pies
Friand Sanflorian (or *de Saint Flour*) Puff pastry pie with pork sausage meat
Potée Auvergnate a stew of salt pork, sausages and cabbage
Langues de mouton aux navets sheep's tongues with turnips
Matelots freshwater fish stews

Cèpes à la crème boletus mushrooms cooked with cream
Coq au vin chicken casserole cooked with bacon, mushrooms red wine

Lyonnais

Lyon is referred to in *Larousse Gastronomique* as the 'gastronomic capital of France'. Its epicurian traditions go back to Roman times, drawing on an abundance of excellent foodstuffs from the surrounding area. Native Lyonnais even indulge in cooked breakfasts in the local bistros, feasting on local specialities like *andouillettes*, *gras-double* (tripe) and *tête de cochon* (pig's head)!

Specialities

Good vegetables, in particular potatoes and onions
Poulardes de Bresse Bresse poultry, the most famous in France
Fish from the rivers, including pike, eels and trout
Frogs' legs and crayfish
Guinea fowl and other game birds
Pork products: *rosette de porc* or *saucisse de Lyon* a hard, dry sausage like a very coarse salami, *tête de cochon pistachée* pig's head brawn with pistachio nuts
Cheese: *Bresse Bleu* possibly the best-known imitation of gorgonzola
Mont d'Or a cousin of the German Munster cheese
Rigottes small, round cheeses made from a mixture of cow's and goat's milk

Some dishes

Matelote d'anguille eel in red wine with onions
Friture fried whitebait from the Rhône
Morue à la Lyonnaise boiled, flaked salt cod fried with onions in butter
Poulet demi-deuil chicken poached in white wine
Poulet aux écrevisses chicken with crayfish-tail sauce
Quenelles financière dumplings with giblets, sweetbreads, mushrooms, truffles
Tripe or *Gras-double à la Lyonnaise* tripe fried in butter with chopped onion

Omelette à la Lyonnaise omelette with onions and chopped parsley

Bugnes (fritters), *matefaims* (thick pancakes), *panges de romans* (a sweet yeast bun), *gâteaux de noix* (walnut cakes)

Savoie

On the mountain pastures cattle are kept for meat and dairy products, while the sunnier hillsides are given over to vines and orchards of cherry, plum, pear and cider apple trees. As in many areas of France, there are walnuts and chestnuts in abundance. Game and fish from the rivers are excellent ingredients for many local dishes.

Specialities

Smoked mountain ham and sausages

Cheeses: *Reblochon* (a soft cheese made from ewe's milk)

Gruyère de Beaufort (a fine imitation of Swiss Gruyère)

Emmental (like Swiss Emmental)

Tomme de Savoie (also called *Tomme de Marc* or *Tomme de Raisins; this is a hard, round cheese with a rind covered with dried grape skins and pips)*

Vacherin (with a very hard rind but an interior so soft that it can be eaten with a spoon

Some dishes

Truite bleue, truite meunière trout steamed, trout fried

Quenelles au gratin dumplings baked in a sauce

Gratin Savoyard alternate layers of potatoes and cheese baked in the oven

Omelette Savoyard potato and cheese omelette

Courgettes à la crème courgettes in cream sauce

Écrevisses au gratin crayfish baked in cream and cheese sauce

Civet de lièvre casserole of hare cooked with wine and hare's blood

Ragoût de veau casserole of veal

Nouilles egg noodles, from Albertville and Chambery in particular

Gâteau de Savoie a light sponge cake

Dauphiné

Lying between Savoie and Provence, bordered on the west by the River Rhône, the region has a climate suitable for fruit, early vegetables and wines, while in the south olives grow readily. The mountain pastures of the interior are a natural source of rich milk and honey. The lakes and small rivers hold excellent stocks of fish and the woods are rich in edible mushrooms.

Specialities

Cheeses: *St. Marcellin* (soft creamy), *Picodon* (goat's milk cheese made in earthenware pots)
Champoleon (a hard mountain cheese made from skimmed milk)
Chartreuse liqueurs, green (the stronger) and yellow, made by the monks of the order of St. Bruno at Voiron since the 16th century
Nougat from Montélimar

Some dishes

Tournedos dauphinois fillet beef with wild mushrooms
Ecrevisses au gratin crayfish baked over with a cheese sauce
Pommes de terre dauphinoise sliced potato in layers with cheese, butter and milk, topped with cheese and baked in the oven
Ravioli
Deffarde de Die sheep's trotters, belly and tripe
Omelette aux truffes truffle omelette

Gascony

This is a region with a coastline rich in fish and forests in the interior full of game. Much poultry is raised, usually on a large-scale commercial basis, while pig farming plays an equally large part in the agricultural scene.

Specialities

Ducks, geese and chickens (the succulent, fat chicken fed on maize for which France is famous)

Black turkeys (sold all over France)
Langue fumee (smoked tongue)
Confit d'oie and *confit de porc* (potted goose and potted pork)
Bayonne ham (a raw, smoked ham, famous throughout the world)
Oysters and mussels from the Bassin d'Arcachon
Izarra liqueur, a Basque speciality, yellow or green
Armagnac, a fine brandy of the Armagnac region
Fruits preserved in Armagnac (prunes, tangerines, raspberries, cherries, etc)
Pavés de Gave (Sweets which are imitations of pebbles from the mountain streams of the Pyrenees)

Some dishes
Paupiettes de dinde stuffed, rolled slices of turkey
Garbure a rich vegetable broth, often with pieces of bacon or ham
Estouffat a stew of haricot beans and pork
Poulet au champagne chicken cooked in champagne
Aillade a garlic sauce served with cold meat and fish
Tournedos thick slices of fillet beef, grilled or fried, garnished in various ways
Soupe aux poissons fish soup

Languedoc, Roussillon, Comte de Foix

Being a region that has been under both Roman and Arab influence, the cuisine of this area still shows signs of its early heritage. The prototype of *cassoulet*, for example, was probably a Roman dish of mutton with white beans (*Larousse Gastronomique*). The cattle and poultry are excellent, especially the ubiquitous goose and duck. Saltwater and freshwater fish play an important part in the cooking of the region. The quality and abundance of fruit and vegetables reflect the superb climate.

Some specialities
Fruits of all kinds, especially cherries, peaches, apples and desert grapes
Vegetables, e.g. asparagus, tomatoes, onions and garlic, peppers, aubergines

Geese, ducks and capons from the Toulouse area
Quails, woodcock and waterfowl from the coastal regions of the Mediterranean
Hare and rabbit from the Cevennes
Hams from Les Montagnes Noirs and Ariège
Mussels from the Bassin de Thau. Octopus, Lobsters, tunny fish and mackerel
Cheeses: the famous *Roquefort* from the small village of that name (strong and blue-veined). *Palardon de Ruons* (a goat's milk cheese from Ardèche

Some dishes
Pot-au-feu à la poule farci beef, stuffed chicken and vegetables cooked in broth
Canard à la Bigarade fried or braised duck(ling) with orange sauce
Cassoulet the most famous from Carcassonne, Toulouse and Castelnaudry (bean, pork, mutton and sausage stew)
Pâtés d'oie and *pâtés de caneton* goose and duck liver pâtés
Alicuit or *alicot* ragout of chicken, turkey and/or goose giblets
Daube Languedocienne braised beef cooked with bacon, ham, vegetables
Soupe de poisson and *bouillabaisse* on the coast, fish soup and casserole of fish, shellfish, vegetables and herbs
Frittons de porc and *f. d'oie* tiny pieces of pork or goose remaining after the fat has been rendered. Made into a paste and eaten as an hors d'oeuvres

Provence

Provence is the land of sunshine and good living, with dishes which match the atmosphere. The basis of cooking *à la Provençale* is a mixture of tomato and garlic usually with olives and olive oil but sometimes garlic by itself. Naturally, with such a long coastline, the region is rich in fish and shellfish, while there is a great deal of game from the forests of the interior.

Specialities
Oysters (prairies and *oursins*)

Mussels, sea urchins (made into a soup called *oursinade*)
Fish, sardines, sole, turbot, tunny, red mullet, clams, octopus, crabs, sea-perch, cod
Olives, grown extensively, producing green and black olives and excellent olive oil
Fruit: cherries and figs, apples, pears and peaches
Candied fruits
Pastries and sweetmeats

Some dishes
Salade Niçoise—potatoes, string beans, anchovies, olives, capers, tomatoes
Poulpe provençal octopus with chopped onion, garlic and white wine
Loup au fenouille sea bass with fennel
Rougets au romarin red mullet with rosemary
Pissaladière a tart with anchovies, onions, tomatoes and olives
Aigo-saou fish soup
Pistou vegetable soup with basil, fennel and garlic
Poulet sauté au tomates lightly fried chicken with tomatoes

8. SHOPS AND SHOPPING

Shopping at home, to most of us, is more often than not a tiresome chore. On holiday, and in a foreign country, shopping becomes once again an exciting adventure. Food shopping in particular, in a country like France where the purchase of good and varied food is pursued with great dedication, is not an inevitable evil but a recurrent pleasure! Since the pleasurability of any new experience tends to be enhanced by doing a small amount of advance homework, here is an introduction to a number of essential shops and to some of the things they sell.

La Charcuterie (Pork butcher/delicatessen)

The strict description of this shop is that of 'pork butcher', specializing not only in pork but in delicatessen made from pork meat and from other parts of the pig. Most *charcutiers* do sell products made from the meat and entrails of other animals, but the main ingredient is pork.

This is where you head when you want to buy things for picnics or cold meals. Depending on the skill of the *charcutier* and the local demand for his products, you will find a wide range of *terrines* and *pâtés* (see below), different kinds of ham, brawn, pies and *quiches*, and many ready-made dishes that can be reheated, like *tomates farcies* (tomatoes with meat filling), *blanquette de veau* (cubed veal in savoury white sauce), *paella* and roast chicken. It is impossible to list everything that might be found in a *charcuterie*, and, of course, the selection changes from region to region. You just have to go along and look at what is on offer, and select what you think you will enjoy. This is one kind of shop which does not appear to have suffered too badly from the growth of the supermarket, since so much depends on the skill of the individual *charcutier*, who may make a veritable art of presenting and decorating his products. You will not find his wares cheap, though, especially if he has made great efforts to produce an imaginative variety of dishes.

Don't expect to find outstanding *charcuterie* in the less frequented areas of the country. The best ones are in the towns, where the population has the money to indulge in fine cuisine.

Glossary

Andouille a cooked sausage, eaten cold and sliced, made from any of all of the following: pig's tripe, calf's tripe, bacon, ham and selected spices. The English translation, as found on French menus, is 'chitterling sausage'!

Andouillette a small version of *Andouille,* fried and eaten hot

Ballottine a kind of *galantine* (see below)

Barquettes oval-shaped pastry cases filled with a savoury *ragoût* of meat, poultry or fish

Boudin black pudding, a great delicacy in France and definitely worth trying

Brochettes any kind of cubed meat on skewers, including liver, kidney and sweetbreads

Fromage de tête pork brawn, or more specifically 'pig's head' brawn

Galantine a dish of pressed, boned meat or poultry (chicken, duck, rabbit, possibly with bacon, liver and ham) cooked in a metal or earthenware dish and surrounded by jelly. It is usually eaten cold (See also *ballottine, terrine, pâté*)

Hure potted pig's head, similar to *fromage de tête,* which is sometimes flavoured with pastachio nuts or truffles

Jambon cru (or *sec*) raw, smoked ham; varieties include *jambon de Bayonne, jambon de Toulouse,* or simple *jambon de Campagne*

Jambon cuit cooked ham, usually labelled as *jambon de Paris, jambon glacé* or *jambon de York*

Jambon persillé flaked ham in jelly, made with a lot of parsley

Museau de boeuf sliced ox muzzle in vinaigrette sauce with onions and parsley

Pâté strictly speaking a pie, i.e. a pastry case filled with a meat, fish, or poultry filling, but now generally accepted as meaning a *terrine* (see below). *Charcuteries* usually offer a large selection: *pâté de campagne* (coarse country pâté), *pâté de canard* (duck pâté), *pâté de foie gras* (smooth goose liver pâté), *pâté de lapin au cognac* (rabbit pâté with brandy), to name but a few

Pâté en croute pâté in a pastry case

Pied de porc boiled pig's trotter; sometimes in vinaigrette sauce

Rillettes a fairly coarse but spreadable paste made of pork meat and fat, seasoned and spiced. It is sometimes a mixture of pork and goose; if you do not like the goose part, ask for *pur porc*. *Rillettes* are usually sold ready potted in plastic containers, with a sealing layer of fat on top. *Rillettes du Mans* are the best known variety

Salades Charcuteries sell dressed salads, and sometimes have an enormous selection. Some of the more common ones are:

Artichauts artichokes
Betteraves beetroot
Carottes râpées grated carrots
Champignons à la grecque button mushrooms in a spicy sauce
Chou rouge dressed red cabbage
Concombre cucumber
Haricot verts green (French) beans
Olignons à la grecque button onions in a spicy sauce
Pommes de terre potato salad

Saucisses sausages for cooking/frying/grilling, usually hanging up or coiled by the metre. They are mostly made of pork and pork fat, but are certainly all meat and have no 'rusk' or 'cereal binder'. *Saucisse de Toulouse* is coarse in texture and unsmoked; *saucisse de campagne* is lightly smoked and spicy, containing pork, beef, pepper, pimento, garlic and herbs. It is poached in water or cooked in thick soups. *Saucisse chipolata* is a thin, unsmoked sausage, probably closest to our English pork chipolatas. It is grilled or fried in small pieces and used to garnish dishes. *Saucisse fumée* is semi-coarse and fairly heavily smoked, but not heavily spiced. It can be poached in water or cooked in *choucroute* or potato dishes. *Saucisses de Strasbourg* are a type of Frankfurter sausage.

Saucisson the kind of sausage, like salami, that is sliced and eaten cold. *Saucissons* are almost exclusively made of pork; many are fairly coarse and air-dried, like *saucisson de Lyon* and *saucisson de montagne*

Tarte à l'oignon onion tart, which can be bought by the piece and eaten hot or cold

Terrine named after the earthenware dish in which it is cooked, it is very much the same as a *galantine* (see above) and also very much the same as a *pâté* (see above). *Terrine* and *pâté* seem to be used fairly indiscriminately to describe the same thing

La Boucherie (Butcher's shop)

The butcher's shop deals in all manner of raw meat, including game and poultry. If it is a *boucherie-charcuterie*, which is very frequently the case, it also sells pork. As in the *charcuterie*, the cuts and prices of all products are displayed on the wall. Prices are usually per kilo (*prix au kg*), but that does not mean that you could not have a very small quantity of something, say 100 grams (*cent grammes*). French meat is characterised by an almost entire absence of fat, so that you will be paying for pure meat. The French butcher is an artist at his trade and will delight in going to some considerable trouble in selecting and cutting for you exactly what you want. The cuts of meat differ from those commonly known in this country, since the animals are cut up differently. Unless you aim at something very straightforward like pork chops or fillet steak, it is always better to tell the butcher what you want the meat for (*pour rôtir, pour griller, pour frire, pour le ragoût de boeuf*, e.g. for roasting, grilling, frying, beef stew).

Glossary

Agneau lamb (not mutton, but very young lamb!)
- *Gigot d'agneau* leg of lamb
- *Carré d'agneau* loin of lamb
- *Épaule d'agneau* shoulder of lamb
- *Côtelette d'agneau* lamb cutlet
- *Noisette d'agneau* or *médaillon d'agneau* fillet cut into a thick, round piece
- *foie d'agneau* lamb's liver

Mouton mutton, or what commonly goes for lamb at home

Boeuf beef
- *Contre-filet* or *faux-filet* sirloin or rump steak
- *Entrecote* rib steak (literally 'between the ribs')
- *Filet de boeuf* (or *tournedos*, or *médaillon*) fillet steak
- *Bifteck* a slice of *contre-filet* or *entrecôte* for grilling
- *Bifteck haché* minced beef. Not usually on show but minced to order
- *Paupiettes de boeuf* beef olives. Sometimes sold ready made
- *Chateaubriand* porterhouse steak

Veau veal
- *Côte de veau* veal chop
- *Escalope de veau* veal fillet, cut very thin

Filet de veau veal loin
Jarret de veau calf's knuckle
Paupiettes de veau veal olives
Foie de veau calf's liver
Riz de veau sweetbreads

Rognons kidneys
Volaille poultry
Poulet chicken. Ask for a *poulet à rôtir* unless you want a boiling fowl
Poussin very small, young chicken
Poularde large roasting chicken, about 2 kilograms in weight
Oie goose
Canard duck
Dindon turkey
Pintadeau, pintade (young) guinea fowl
Caille quail
Faisan pheasant
Lapin rabbit
Chevreuil venison

La Boulangerie/Patisserie (Baker's shop)

The baker's shop is probably the most important shop of all in France, since bread is such a major ingredient in the French diet. Typical French white bread, which, incidentally, is made with sour dough, is best eaten fresh (in fact, it can hardly be eaten at all when it is stale!). Therefore, the *boulanger* bakes twice a day — except Sundays and Mondays. (see 'Shopping Hours'). You can rely on fresh bread early in the morning and late in the afternoon in most places. A *dépot de pain* is a shop, usually an *épicerie*, sometimes a *charcuterie*, which sells bread but does not make it. If you cannot find a baker, look for this sign.

The commonest French bread is made in rolled loaves, long and thin, ranging from the thinnest *ficelle* ('length of string') and the somewhat thicker *flute* (actually fatter than a flute!) to the substantial *baguette* ('stick'). There are many others, some more interestingly shaped, like the *couronne* (crown), which is round with a hole in the middle, and the attractive *épi*, which looks like a large ear of corn. Fancy shapes are usually more expensive than plain ones, but the price of all bread is laid down by law, and a price list is hanging up in every bakery.

Apart from standard white bread most *boulangeries* also sell rye bread (*pain de seigle*), wholemeal bread (*pain complet*), rolls (*petit pains*), *brioches* (rolls made of a rich yeast dough containing butter and eggs) and, of course, the well-known *croissants* (crescent-shaped rolls made of puff pastry). Often you will also find simple *patisseries* like *pain aux raisins* (currant buns) or *tarte aux pommes* (apple tart) in a boulangerie, but this is more likely if the shop is a combined *boulangerie-pâtisserie*, which is frequently the case. A shop which is only a *pâtisserie*, on the other hand, does not sell any bread at all.

The French are justly famous for their pastries and tarts, and every town, if not village, has at least one first-class *pâtisserie*. Some of these things are very expensive; a sizeable fruit tart can cost £3-4 (33-45F). Apart from apples, the most common types of fruit used for *tartes* are *abricots* (apricots), *fraises* (strawberries), *framboises* (raspberries) and, in the summer months, in regions where they grow, *myrtilles* (blueberries). For about 4.00F you get a *tartelette*, a small tart, which is just nice as a sampler. Then there are cream cakes and small iced cakes (*petits fours*) and simpler things like *croissants* filled with marzipan, nuts or chocolate cream. Frequently, the *pâtissier* also makes his own chocolates and small confectionaries (labelled *Produit de maison* i.e. 'home-made') and sells chocolate, sweets and glacé fruits of other manufacture. These things are not cheap, to say the least!

L'Épicerie/Alimentation Générale (Grocer's Shop)

Every small village has its *épicerie*, its grocer's shop, which sells a wide range of products from tinned and packaged food to wine, milk, *charcuteries*, cheese and even bread. Many are part of a chain like Spar, or Économats, or Co-op, or whatever the chain established in that particular region happens to be, and frequently, despite their diminutive size, they are self-service, so that language problems are not likely to be an issue.

Milk (le lait)

Milk is not delivered to the door but is sold in cartons or plastic bottles in grocers, dairies and supermarkets. Since it comes in at least three varieties, it is a good idea to look closely at the carton: U.H.T. is long-life milk, *lait demi-écrémé* is skimmed milk, and *lait entier* is what you probably want, i.e. fresh, whole milk. There is also *lait battu* (or *lait du beurre*), and if you put that into your coffee you will not like it one bit, because it is buttermilk.

Butter (le beurre)

Butter comes in many brands and price ranges. Most of it is fresh, i.e. unsalted, some makes are lightly salted (*salé*). The most expensive *beurre de table* from Normandy can cost 50% more than the cheapest brand, which is still very good quality butter. For cooking, buy *beurre cuisinier*.

Cheeses (*les fromages*)

There are so many cheeses to choose from in France (over 300, according to some authorities) that one could eat a different cheese every day. Some are well known abroad, because they are widely exported, others will be a new experience and can add an interesting dimension to eating if you are buying your own food. A little experimentation can do no harm.

As a general rule, you should look for cheeses with a high fat content as they are the tastiest, being made from full-cream milk. The *matière grasse* in the better cheeses will range from 45% to 75%. Cheeses with less than 40% fat content, which is not uncommon in fresh cheeses and cheese preparations, are made from skimmed milk. It definitely pays to read the label carefully. The higher the fat content, the higher the price of the cheese, of course.

Most famous of all French cheeses is probably *'Monsieur' Camembert*, as he is whimsically known. Originating in Normandy, it was invented by a local farmer's wife in 1790 in the village of Vimoutiers, where there is a statue of the good lady to commemorate the fact. *Camembert* is now made all over France and even in other countries, but the best is recognised as coming from Normandy, so look for the place of origin on the label. French law demands that the maker must state where his product is made. A cheese similar to Camembert in character is *Reblochon*, which has the same round shape but an orange-yellow crust. To the same family of mild, creamy cheeses covered in white 'noble' fungus belongs *Coulommiers*, and of course *Brie*, which comes in rounds as big as dinner plates. *Brie* is a very ancient cheese, certainly known in the 15th century. It was originally made in the area of Brie, just east of Paris. It should be eaten just before it starts to run to be at its best. *Pont l'Evêque* is square and sold in boxes like Camembert, but it has a yellow crust and is much more pungent.

If you like a hard, fairly salty cheese try *Comté*, the French equivalent to Swiss *Gruyère*. It has the same nutty taste, but the holes are slightly smaller. Another hard cheese is *Cantal*, which some people say is similar to mild Cheddar.

The most popular blue cheese are *Roquefort*, *Bleue des Causses*, *Bleue d'Auvergne* and *Bresse Bleue*. *Roquefort* vies with *Camembert* as France's most famous cheese, but it is rather more 'special', not only because it is unique to one area of France, the *causses* (limestone plateaux) to the south of the Massif Central, but also because it is very expensive and, on account of this and its very concentrated, tangy taste, is not eaten in large quantities. It is made wholly of ewe's milk, whereas *Bleue des Causses*, *Bleue d'Auvergne*, and *Bresse Bleue* are made of cow's milk and are, therefore, milder.

Port Salut and *St. Paulin*, both made by monks and very similar to each other in taste and appearance, are round, semi-hard cheeses with a smooth, buttery flavour and a yellow, almost fungus-free crust. *Tome de Raisins* is a white, solid, mild-flavoured cheese, the chief attraction of which lies in its black rind of dried grape skins and pips.

Then there are innumerable goat's cheeses, *fromages de chèvre*, which are strictly for bold palates. There is the dark-grey, pyramid-shaped *Levroux* and its smaller brother, the *Valençay*, the Provençal *Banons*, which are wrapped in herb leaves and tied up with raffia, the cylindrical *Saint-Maure* and scores of others, many of them purely local, made by small farmers in small quantities. They are nearly all small and round, often fairly repulsive looking, with a very strong, distinctive flavour which in some varieties resembles goat's dung rather more closely than goat's milk. In shops and markets goat's cheeses are frequently set out on straw matting.

At the opposite end of the scale are the *Petits Suisses*, little fresh cream cheeses usually sold in packs of six or eight. They come either plain (to be eaten with sugar) or in fruit flavours and are so small that one of them just makes one delicious mouthful. They are extremely popular with the French, as is *fromage blanc* (smooth cream cheese sold in margarine-size tubs) which is eaten with sugar sprinkled on the top.

La Crémerie (Dairy)

There seem to be fewer dairies around these days than there were, obviously the result of modern packaging methods and supermarket techniques. The *crémerie* is the good, old-fashioned dairy where butter is sold off the block and smelly cheeses as big as wagon-wheels are lined up on the counter. In big or medium-sized, prosperous towns with a discriminating clientele there is still a demand for the specialised *crémerie*, and it is a feast for eyes and nose to take a look round one. Butter, yoghurt and cream are now generally sold pre-packed, but cheeses reveal themselves in their vigorous, unabashed entirety. The advantage of buying in a *crémerie* is the fantastic selection and the freshness of the products. The assistant may even let you have a *dégustation* (a taste) of a few kinds of cheese before you make up your mind. It must be said, though, that the large *hypermarchés* offer a comparable selection, including many cheeses which can be bought off the piece, and their prices are much lower.

La Quincaillerie (Ironmonger)

The ironmonger sells everything from pots and pans to nails, screws and paints. He also, very frequently, sells a good selection of everyday glass and tableware. Such shops are often veritable aladdin's caves, fun to browse through and revealing unexpected ideas for gifts to take home.

La Droguerie

There is no strictly correct translation for this. One could say that it is a cross between a chemist and an ironmongers (except that it sells no medicines!). If you want a map or a plastic bucket, a comb, a bar of soap, hair shampoo, ant killer, clothes pegs, a tube of adhesive or a hook for the bathroom wall, *la droguerie* is the place to go.

La Pharmacie (Chemist)

This is what we call a 'dispensing chemist', where you buy

medicines on prescription as well as proprietary medicines and those which may be sold without a prescription. We have found over the years that quite a few items which one could not get without a prescription at home fall into this latter category. Pharmacists in France are very serious people, very professional in their white coats, and almost as enigmatic as doctors themselves. If you have a fairly minor complaint like a sore throat, mild tonsilitis, hayfever, an allergy rash or a sunburn you can happily entrust yourself to the pharmacist's vast knowledge and rely on him selling you something (usually very expensive) which will be effective and save you a visit to the surgery. Bear in mind that health insurances, whether private or through the DHSS, do not refund the cost of medicines bought without a doctor's prescription (see also 'Dealing with Illness', p.144).

La pharmacie is also the place to go if you want expert information on edible and poisonous mushrooms. Since collecting fungi is such a popular pastime in France, chemists in holiday areas have taken it upon themselves to instruct the public in 'fungus recognition'. Many chemists display large posters in the window or inside the shop and sell, or hand out free, booklets and leaflets which describe the most commonly found edible and poisonous fungi. If you have collected a basketful but are not quite sure, take them to the *pharmacie* to have them identified. Pharmacies in holiday areas are also experts on snakes, especially venomous ones, of which several species roam the country and do occasionally bite people! A *pharmacie* will not only display snake posters and even show tanks of live snakes in the window, but will sell you a 'survival kit' of syringe and anti-snake-bite-serum to take with you on your outings in the countryside.

Incidentally, *comprimés* are tablets, *gouttes* are drops, and *suppositoires* are suppositories for insertion at the posterior end. The French are very fond of this method of application, but if you are not, decline the pharmacist's suggestion politely. Do not wait until you are outside the shop to discover that you have bought something which you are never going to use!

Things like *pansements* (plasters of the first-aid type), *coton hydrophile* (cotton wool) and *serviettes hygiéniques* (sanitary towels) can also be bought at the supermarket.

La Papeterie (Stationers)

This is the stationers, often combined with a bookshop to make a *librarie-papeterie*. The *papeterie* sells pens, pencils, postcards, writing paper and envelopes, newspapers and magazines, maps, guides and games. It does not sell stamps, but usually stocks a few for purchasers of postcards.

Le Tabac

This word is short for *le bureau de tabac*, the tobacconist. The tobacconist is also very frequently the newsagent, and this is the place to go to if you want to buy stamps but do not fancy queueing at the post office. The tabac also sells lottery tickets, car licences, parking discs and, sometimes, postcards and souvenirs. The shop sign looks like a large, red cigar.

La Blanchisserie (Laundry)

If your hotel has no laundry facilities you may have to take a few things to the laundry, who will usually take at least two days to return them. *Blanchisseries* (or *laveries*) *automatiques libre-service*, i.e. launderettes, are unfortunately not very common in France except on campsites, in resorts geared to foreign tourists and in holiday villages. If you need one, the local tourist office may come up with an answer.

Le Nettoyage à Sec/Le Pressing (Dry Cleaner)

The dry-cleaner, as at home, offers a variety of services other than dry-cleaning, such as repairs, alterations and pressing (hence the name). In *hypermarchés* one can usually find a one- or two-hour dry cleaning service, which comes in very handy on holiday.

Le Coiffeur (Hairdresser)

Le coiffeur (*pour*) *dames* is the hairdresser, *le coiffeur* (*pour*) *hommes* the barber. It is always something of a frightening experience to go to the hairdressers in any foreign country if you have only a modest command of the language. Hairdressing is a ceremony with its own vocabulary. Your dictionary fails to inform you of the French equivalent of a 'shampoo and set' or a 'blow wave'. But fear not, in France all the principal procedures and their prices are exhibited in the window and once again inside the shop. So you can work it all out standing outside the shop, including whether you can afford to go in at all. And if words fail you trying to describe a hair-style, use your hands. Simply give a graphic description of a crew cut, or whatever, and say firmly '*comme ça*!' 15% service is always included in the advertised price.

Glossary
Shampooing shampoo
Mise en plis set
Coupe cut
Coupe entretien trim
Coupe classique (*hommes*) (men's) standard haircut; the French equivalent of short back and sides
Cheveux courts short hair
Cheveux longs long hair. A shampoo and set for long hair is more expensive than one for short hair
Brushing blow-wave, blow-drying
Permanente permanent wave
Colorant tinting

Marchés (Markets)

Most towns, even small ones, have their *marché*, whether in the open or in *les halles* (under cover), and it is more often than not held on a Saturday. Market day is still the same colourful, noisy, bustling affair that it has always been. There are clothes and shoes, pots and pans, handbags and cheap toys and, above all, farm produce, which somehow appears much more genuine and colourful out in the open air than it does inside a shop. The peaches seem extra large, the chickens are still alive (if you dare!), the eggs still have traces of farmyard dirt on them. Old ladies have brought along a few bunches of carrots or onions which they have grown in their back gardens. There is the nut vendor standing behind a mountain of sugared almonds, which disappear as fast as they are heaped up. As in all good markets, there are cheese stalls and fish stalls and quacking ducks in wooden cages, as well as boxes of baby chicks, ducklings and rabbits to delight the children.

Markets are fun, but it is an error to think that you will necessarily get everything cheaper there than at the supermarket. In fact, unless you are very alert with your mental arithmetic, you are very likely to be short changed by a stall keeper who cannot quite make the effort to get it right!

Supermarchés and Hypermarchés (Supermarkets)

If shopping has to be done in large quantities once a week, the best place to accomplish this with the least fuss and in the shortest time is a *supermarché* or *hypermarché*. Supermarchés are what they are at home: mainly very large self-service food shops with sections for non-food items including pots and tableware, stationery, textiles etc. A *hypermarché* is a very large complex housing not only a large supermarket but other shops as well. Thus, without having to leave the building, one can buy shoes, toys, car accessories, leather goods, pets, electrical goods, camping gear etc. It is normal for *hypermarchés* to also have a sizeable cafeteria, where one can eat a good, varied and reasonably-priced meal in surprisingly pleasant surroundings. These cafeterias are in the habit of being closed for meals between 2.30 p.m. and 6.30 p.m. The advantages of shopping in a *hypermarché* are manyfold:

Vast selection
Low prices
No parking problems
Don't close for lunch (not, unfortunately, an invariable rule)
Open Mondays (as a rule)
Open till late at night, 9 p.m. or later

Hypermarchés and large *supermarchés* are usually well outside town centres, sometimes on industrial estates. Look for hoardings on approach roads to towns advertising them by name and address. Popular names are INTERMARCHÉ, MAMMOUTH, RADAR, ROND POINT (co-op).

Department Stores

Some sort of department store is to be found in most moderate-sized towns. Popular stores, (popular in price, too), which are distributed all over France, are *Monoprix*, *Prisunic* and *Nouvelles Galeries*. They usually have a food department and, in larger towns, a cafeteria.

Shopping Hours

With the exception of *supermarchés* and *hypermarchés*, most of which are open from Monday through Saturday (some smaller ones may be closed Monday morning), most food shops can be expected to be closed on Monday: either all day Monday, or Monday a.m. or Monday p.m., there seems to be no general rule. The best thing to do is to check on opening times *before the weekend*, or to discount Monday as a shopping day altogether. Even butchers and bakers who, by tradition are the most hard working shopkeepers and have the longest opening hours, will not sacrifice their day-off or half-day off to the ever-hungry. Non-food shops are more likely to be open on a Monday, and the baker is more likely to be open at least on Monday morning than the butcher(!).

As for Sunday opening, this is completely haphazard and depends largely on demand. One may find a butcher or a baker open on a Sunday morning, and in busy tourist resorts all sorts of shops may be doing a brisk trade all Sunday.

Banks in some localities are closed all Monday, in others on Saturday. In towns where Saturday is market day, the *Crédit Agricole*, which is by no means just a 'Farmers' Bank' and has probably the largest number of branches of any bank throughout France, is always open on Saturdays. All banks are closed on Sunday! Post offices are open six days a week and don't usually close for lunch. In big towns the main post office opens on Sunday morning.

Opening hours for food shops are generally from 8 a.m. (or earlier) till 12 noon, and after lunch from 2 p.m. till 6.30 or 7.00 p.m. Some, especially butchers, may not re-open after lunch until 2.30 or 3 p.m. and remain open till 7 or 8 p.m. You are most likely to find long lunch hours and late-night opening in the hot, southern regions of France in the summer. It saves much frustration to keep these lunchtime closing hours in mind when planning to shop for a midday picnic! *Hypermarchés* and most larger *supermarchés*, of course, do not close for lunch, but you may be a long way from one when your stomach reminds you of the time of day. Banking hours are very much like shopping hours, but banks close earlier in the afternoon, at 4 or 5 p.m. In Paris, banks tend to open at 9 a.m.

Roadside stalls

In the larger fruit and wine growing areas the products of the countryside (fruit, wine, cheese, honey) are often offered for sale by the roadside. Prices have to be carefully compared with supermarket and shop prices, since such outlets do not always offer bargains. A *dégustation* (tasting) may be a very tempting invitation, but if you accept it you should sample very critically before you load a dozen bottles of mediocre wine into your car.

Itinerant Salesmen

A part of the French scene, especially during the tourist months, are the itinerant salesmen from North Africa and others parts of that continent who offer their wares in prominent places on the streets. Occasionally, bargains in the way of native jewellery, sculpture and leatherware are to be had, but one should inspect things critically and, above all, be prepared to bargain with the vendor. This is not only possible but expected, and even our small daughter has managed to get some very attractive necklaces for considerably less than the price asked (and, one might add, at a fraction of the price asked for the same thing in a fashionable boutique elsewhere). While you cannot rely on getting a bargain in such a situation, it is a bit of fun, and you can sometimes buy unusual things which are not readily available elsewhere.

9. WINES, SPIRITS AND BEER

Wines

France is one of the world's great producers of wine, second only in volume of production to Italy. Most of the 65 million or so hectolitres of wine produced a year is consumed in France itself.

The main wine-growing regions of the country are:

Champagne	Provence
Alsace	Languedoc-Roussillon
Jura	Cahors
Chablis	Gaillac
Loire Valley	Bordeaux
Burgundy (incl. Beaujolais)	Bergerac
Côtes du Rhône	Savoie

All these regions produce fine wines and table wines, which are extensively known abroad. Perhaps the most famous are those of Champagne, Bordeaux and Burgundy (including Beaujolais).

Two further areas produce a great deal of wine, Cognac and Armagnac, the larger proportion of which is converted into the two types of brandy known by those names.

There are extensive vineyards in other areas of France, but not to any significant extent in regions north of the Loire (except Champagne and Alsace), the bleaker parts of the Massif Central and the high altitudes of the Alps and the Pyrenees.

The best wines of France are classed '*Appellation Contrôlée*', which is a term only permitted to be used after the French Ministry of Agriculture has been satisfied that a wine is produced under conditions which are strictly defined by law. The system was set up properly in 1935 to prevent unscrupulous producers who made inferior wines from passing them off as great ones by naming them so, e.g. Burgundy or Bordeaux.

The system has only rarely been abused since, and the term *Appellation Contrôlée* may be taken as a guarantee that the wine so labelled does actually come from the place named on the bottle,

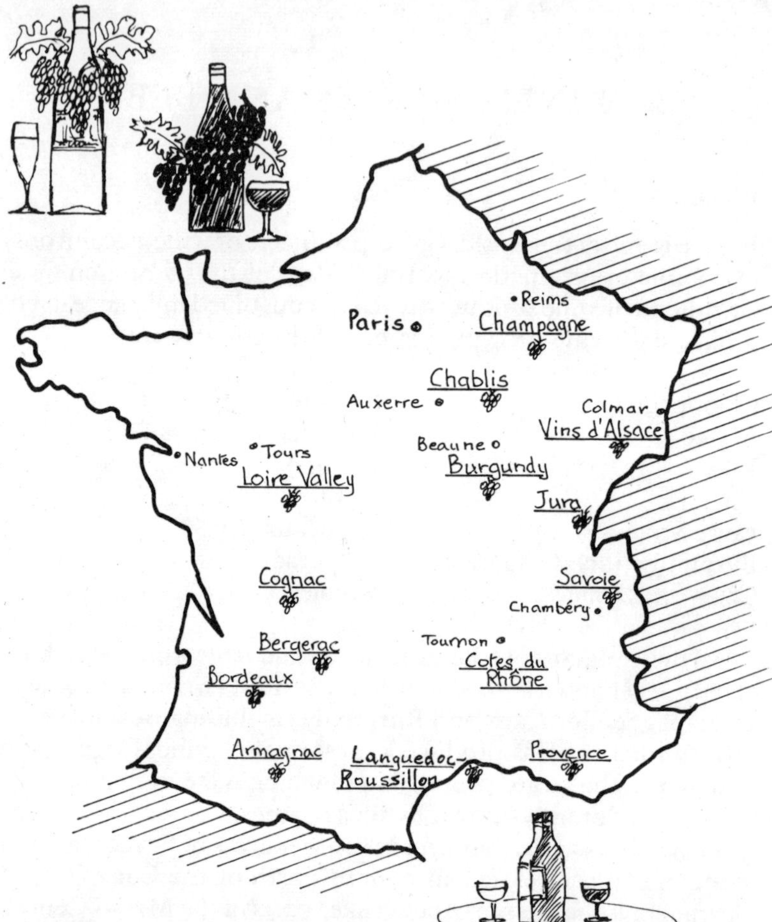

The Wine Growing Regions of France

There are further large areas of vineyards in other parts of the country, but none exist north of the Loire and on the more rugged parts of the Massif Central.

Note: Black and white grapes in the diagram indicate that both red and white wines are produced.

that it has been made from grapes grown on specific vines grown in specific types of soil, that it has been made by an approved process and has a minimum degree of alcohol content. The term does not imply a criterion of quality as such, but such controls inevitably result in quality, which is further safeguarded by limiting the maximum production of wine per hectare to prevent a lowering of quality by over-cultivation.

The term *Appellation Contrôlée* may be applied to a region, a sub-region or a *commune*, which means that the label on a bottle of, say, Bordeaux, may not simply say *Appellation Bordeaux Contrôlée* but, for example, *Appellation St. Emilion Contrôlée* or *Appellation Graves Contrôlée*, which makes life none the easier for the uninitiated, who are simply looking for the name of the region somewhere on the label. Fortunately all Bordeaux wines come in distinctive round-shouldered bottles, which helps to identify them. Bottle labels are altogether a confusing subject. Some top Burgundy and Bordeaux wines are graded into *crus*, i.e. 'growths', according to their prestige rating. In Burgundy the grades are *Grand Cru* and *Premier Cru*. For the Médoc wines of Bordeaux the rating goes from *Premier Crus* (first growth) to *Cinquième Cru* (fifth growth), but the bottle label may simply say *Cru Classé* or *Grand Cru Classé*, which can be any one of the five. Below these is the *Cru Bourgeois*, which is of a lower rating. Any label with the word *cru* on it may not bear the term *Appellation Contrôlée* at all, but it is implied, and the price will leave you in no doubt as to the standing of that particular wine!

The right to use the term *Appellation Contrôlée*, is naturally greatly prized by wine producers, and many strive to be recognised. For those who do not quite reach the required standards of production there is a second rank, so to speak. After inspection, a producer may be allowed to use the term *Vin Delimité de Qualité Supérieure* (abbreviated V.D.Q.S.). Many of these wines are quite excellent and should not be ignored in favour of *Appellation Contrôlée* wines. In fact, many of them eventually advance into the A.C. ranks.

Finally, there is a third category, recently introduced to encourage the improvement of many wines which have, up till now, been regarded as inferior. This is the denomination *Vin de Pays*. These unassuming wines are often very good and certainly to be recommended for use as table wines for everyday drinking, particularly as they are at the lower end of the price scale.

France produces both red and white wines: about two-thirds of the total output is red, one-third white. Among the red wines, those from Bordeaux and Burgundy are the best known. Bordeaux wines, in their distinctive round-shouldered bottles, encompass all the evocative 'Chateaux' labels. Burgundy wines, which are heavier, more full-bodied in character than Bordeaux wines, include the well-known Beaujolais labels, among them the *Beaujolais Supérieur* (a simple Beaujolais with an extra degree of alcohol above the minimum), the *Beaujolais Villages*, which is one grade above a basic Beaujolais, and the top qualities, which go under the names of the communes in which they are produced, e.g. *Fleurie*, *Moulin-a-Vent*, *Julienas*, *Chénas*.

The red wines of the Rhône valley, with their warm, robust, southern character come in popularity not far behind the Bordeaux's and Burgundies. Some famous labels like *Côte Rôtie*, *Chateauneuf du Pape* and *Hermitage* originate here.

Languedoc-Roussillon, or *le Midi*, produces nearly one-third of all the wines grown in France. Few are *A.C.* wines; most are strong, red *vins ordinaires*, *Vins de Pays* or, at best, *V.D.Q.S.* wines, like *Corbières*, *Minervois* or *Costières de Gard*, which one can buy in any supermarket and enjoy without any financial misgivings.

The best-known white wines come from Alsace (resembling German Rhine and Moselle wines), from the Loire valley (dry wines like *Muscadet*, *Sancerre and Pouilly-Fumé*) sweet wines from Anjou (which also produces the best *rosé*), Bordeaux (dry or medium-sweet *Graves*, sweet *Sauternes* and *Barsac*), Bergerac (*sweet Montbazillac* and *Côtes de Bergerac*), Burgundy (light *Puilly-Fuissé*, down-to-earth *Macon Blanc*) and, of course, *Chablis*.

In a book such as this the authors cannot hope to mention all the many types of wine to emerge from a prolific wine-producing country like France. The best advice we can give is that the reader should acquire Hugh Johnson's Pocket Guide to Wine, which is a veritable mine of information, and, for in-depth study, The World Atlas of Wine, also by Hugh Johnson.

Very few imported wines are seen on sale in France, and when they are, you can be sure that they are more expensive than their French equivalent. It is a difficult person indeed who will not find something that appeals among the vast selection of French-produced wines. Nor is it necessary to spend large sums of money (though you can, if you want to, spend 60F easily on a top bottle of *Médoc*). Leaving aside the really basic, nameless *Vins de Table*, which sell in litre-bottles for as little as 4-5F, a nice Languedoc

Vine de Pays or *V.D.Q.S.* wine might be priced from 5.50F upwards or a bottle of A.C. Bordeaux for twice that, but the latter will not necessarily appeal to you twice as much. Unless you are a real wine connoisseur (and after all how many of us are?) who knows exactly what he wants — which vintage, which year, which *commune* — the best way to make the most of a perplexing situation is to buy half a dozen or so bottles at the beginning of a French holiday and then to stick to the one or two labels you like best. This does not work so well if you tour from region to region or even from town to town, because different shops and supermarkets sell different brands of wine.

Wines can be bought direct from the producers in almost all wine growing areas. You can go to the vintner's *cave* (cellar) and have a tasting (*dégustation*), after which you can purchase bottles to take away. In the case of the very cheapest wines you can even bring your own plastic container to be filled with as many gallons as you think you can drink! Depending on the region, you can get some very passable wines very cheaply from the *cave communal*, but very often the plonk sold in this way is acceptable to the local palate only. Out of six wines we tasted in a co-operative *cave* in Ardèche one year we could not drink a single one! This had, of course, something to do with the type of wine grown in that area which is at best *Vin de Pays*. If you are in a top-quality wine growing area and intend to take a few good bottles home there is an obvious advantage in going to a reputable *cave* and taste before buying. However, one must not expect to get the wine cheaply. If anything it will be more expensive than the equivalent wine bought in a shop or supermarket. After all, the producer has more work selling individual bottles than selling in bulk to a wholesaler, and he naturally tries to take advantage to some extent of the novelty to the tourist of a *cave* visit.

Beware of buying wines from roadside stalls, frequently to be seen on main highways in summer. As likely as not you will get a modest wine at an inflated price.

There are, in most towns, specialist wine shops. One great advantage they have is that they frequently carry a really good range of the better wines. Moreover, you will be able to discuss your purchase with the proprietor, invariably very knowledgeable. Prices in specialist wine shops are generally higher than those in supermarkets and chain grocers, but even they carry ranges of cheaper wines. However, when it comes to spirits, they cannot compete with the sometimes spectacular bargains offered by supermarkets.

In recent years, with an increasing demand on the part of the French themselves and the enormous influx of foreign tourists, the supermarkets have taken the vending of wine more seriously. It is not uncommon now to find that bottles are not simply stacked on shelves or in bins on the floor, but allocated an impressive display along one whole wall, in which the better wines are grouped and appropriately flagged. Special offers are conspicuously publicized. Supermarket prices are keen because of bulk buying, and the wines can usually be relied on for quality, because supermarkets acquire many of their wines from the best shippers and vineyards. Prices of spirits, too, are keenest in supermarkets. You can save as much as 10F on a bottle of brandy and make proportional savings on liqueurs and aperitifs such as *Pernod**.

Glossary

Here are a few useful expressions which turn up repeatedly on labels of wine bottles. We also list some of the best known wines from the main areas. The list is nothing like complete, but we hope it will help in a small way.

Appellation Contrôlée see p.117
V.D.Q.S. Vin Délimité de Qualité Supérieure see p.119
Vin de Pays see p.119
Vin de Table very ordinary wine, not classified
Cru growth, see classification p.119
Mis en bouteille . . . bottled at . . .
Mis (en bouteille) par le propriétaire (or producteur) bottled by the grower
Mis (en bouteille) dans nos caves bottled in our cellars
Mis (en bouteille) au château bottled on the estate

**Pernod* is one of the many brand names under which the potent spirit made from aniseed is sold. It is drunk diluted with water, which turns it a milky white. Regarded mainly as a man's drink, it is a favourite drink in the south, but people are seen drinking it all over France these days.

Négociant shipper; wine merchant
Récolte crop; vintage
Supérieur (after the name of a Bordeaux wine) containing 1° of alcohol above the legal minimum
Commune wine producing parish
Blanc de blancs any wine made from white grapes, usually very dry

Types of Grapes

Do not confuse the names of grapes used in wine making with the names of wines (although in Alsace, as in Germany, wines are most frequently labelled by the type of grape from which they are made). The most commonly grown types of grapes in France are:

Red	*White*
Pinot Noir	Chardonnay
Gamay	Sauvignon Blanc
Caberet Sauvignon	Ugni Blanc
Merlot	Chenin Blanc
Muscat	Pinot Blanc
Grenache	Riesling
	Sylvaner
	Gewürztraminer

Some wines from different regions

Bordeaux

Médoc/Haut Médoc	Graves
St. Estèphe	Sauternes
Pauillac	Entre-deux-Mers
St. Julien	Margaux
St. Emilion	Pomerol
Fronsac	

Burgundy

Côte de Beaune	
(e.g. Pommard, Meursault)	Pouilly-Fuissé
Côte de Nuits	
(e.g. Nuits St. Georges)	Beaujolais (Villages)
Macon (Villages)	Chablis

Loire

Muscadet
Saumur
Sancerre
Coteaux du Layon
Rosé d'Anjou
Touraine
Chinon
Vouvray
Pouilly-Fumé

Rhône Valley

Côtes du Rhone
Chateauneuf du Pape
Tavel
Hermitage

Languedoc-Rousillon

Banyuls (fortified sweet wine)
Fitou
Corbières
Minervois
St. Chinian
Frontignan
Costières de Gard

Spirits

Apart from the universally known brandies of the Cognac region (*Martel*, *Hennessy*, Courvoisier, *Remy Martin* etc.) there are a number of other notable spirits made in France. The best known is Armagnac, a brandy with a flavour totally different from Cognac and made in an entirely different way. From Normandy comes *Calvados*, a kind of brandy made from apple cider, very agreeable and usually cheaper than Cognac or Armagnac.

Prunelle and *Poire William* are clear spirits, one sloe-flavoured, the other distilled from pear juice. *Cointreau* is an orange-flavour liqueur made in Angers. *Grand Marnier*, also a liqueur, comes in two labels: *Cordon Rouge* and *Cordon Jaune*. The latter is sweeter and lower in alcohol. *Bénédictine* is another liqueur made with herbs. *Crème de Menthe* is a peppermint-flavoured liqueur which many non-French find quite revolting.

---

*If you want to take home wines to the UK from France, you can legally import into any other Common Market country, for personal consumption and without duty, 4 litres of wine (roughly 6 ordinary, 0.7 litre bottles) and 1½ litres of spirits. If you decide to forego the allowance of spirits, then your wine allowance, per person over 17 years old, will rise to 7 litres or 10 bottles of 0.7 litres. It is, of course, possible to import a larger quantity, but then you have to declare the amount to the Customs and pay VAT and duty.

The *apéritif*, a long, pre-meal drink comparatively low in alcohol, is much valued in France. Dry vermouth, *Noilly Prat*, or *Chambèry* (from the town of that name) with or without a dash of *cassis* (blackcurrent and brandy cordial) are very popular. Common brand names for apéritifs are *Amer Picon*, *Byrhh*, *Dubonnet*, *Lillet*, and *St. Raphael*. *Pernod* and other aniseed and fennel-flavoured imitations of *absinthe* (banned from sale by law) are widely used as *apéritifs*.

Beer

Beer, purchased in supermarkets by the carton (12 or 24 bottles) is very agreeable and cheap. It can also be bought in one-litre bottles with screw tops. Many well-known brands are available, including Stella Artois and Kronenbourg, bottled by the ¼ litree, and they can cost as little as one third of the price of bottled or canned beers in the UK. If you want to bring them home, there is, at the time of writing, a limit of 48 litres duty free. It's just a matter of coping with all that weight.

French beers are of the lager type, light, but very drinkable, especially chilled. It is better to buy beers brewed in the north of the country, since they are closer in character to what we are used to in the UK.

10. EATING OUT

The opportunity to eat in restaurants is one of the aspects of a visit to France which most people place high on their list of priorities. France has such an outstanding reputation as one of the world's gastronomic Meccas that its restaurants inevitably play a large part in the tourist scene. The French themselves enjoy eating out, especially at weekends, and it is very often, though not necessarily, their custom which determines the culinary standards of an establishment. It is a fallacy, however, to think that just because you are in France, every restaurant you walk into will serve you with a gastronomic experience, or even a meal to remember. You are not likely to find famous dishes and much talked-about regional delicacies on the menu of every motorway pull-in or get a six-course feast for the price of a sandwich. As elsewhere in the world, it all depends on where you eat and what you pay. But anyone who applies a bit of care and forethought to the subject of eating will find France a rewarding hunting ground for good-food lovers. The French do always, after all, try to make their food appetising and interesting.

Self-service restaurants

Self-restaurants, as they are now often referred to, or *restaurants libre-service*, have increased greatly in popularity in recent years, and are now to be found in most larger towns, sometimes as part of a department store or a shopping centre. *Hypermarchés* and large *supermarchés* nearly always have one, often called a *cafeteria*. They are much frequented by the French, who know a good food bargain when they see one. Hypermarket cafeterias are always busy at lunchtime and then again in the evening, when they open from 6.30 p.m. until 9 p.m. or later, because they offer a convenient way of combining the week's shopping with having a bite to eat. Families on holiday with smaller children soon find that they are the answer to their prayers for an eating place where they can feed the children before they fall asleep (which they invariably do by the time a conventional restaurant serves dinner at 8 or 9 p.m.)

As with all restaurants, standards of cuisine in self-service restaurants vary, but from considerable experience we can say that on the whole you get ample, appetizing and satisfying food at a modest price. Furthermore, seating arrangements are usually generous, the decor tasteful and the comfort of a standard seldom found in self-service restaurants at home.

Menus are varied but rarely include soup as a starter (this item seems to be disappearing from many restaurant menus). Starters include various salads (*crudités*) and cold meat such as slices of raw ham, cooked ham pâté or *andouilles* (see p.103). Main courses start around 12.00F for sausages (the Frankfurter type) and chips (*saucisses/frites*) and go to 40.00F for fillet steak, if available. Apart from other examples of the chips-with-everything variety such as *poulet rôti/frites* and *steak/frites*, there are usually three or four *plats du jour* in various price ranges and suiting different tastes, anything from *boeuf bourguignon* with two veg to *couscous*, a North African dish of rice, mutton, chicken and vegetables, which is very popular in France and is sold ready-made in tins.

Typical *desserts* would be fresh fruit salad (*macedoine de fruits*), yoghurt, cream cheese to be eaten with sugar (*fromage blanc*), various fruit tarts and gateaux. The cheese selection is usually limited to two or three more popular kinds like Camembert and Brie. French bread or rolls and butter are always available, though not free! Since bread can more often than not be found in a bin at the *start* of the counter, before you get to the actual food display, it is a good idea to look out for it then rather than remember it when you get to the check-out, which means sending a member of the family all the way back along the queue (which can be very long!).

Many large self-service restaurants make allowances for 'second thoughts' by providing a separate counter, beyond the main check-out, where one can get additional bread, butter, desserts and drinks without having to queue all over again.

Eating in unfamiliar self-service restaurants has its small problems. If you cannot quite figure out what's what and you cannot quickly make up your mind what you want to eat while a long queue of hungry people is pushing up behind you, you may end up like the elderly English lady in 'Le Bordeaux' in Cahors, who was looking down disconsolately upon an anaemic plateful of boiled fish and rice while her husband, in embarrassed merriment, kept saying: 'Well, *you* chose it; *you* eat it . . .'. You would be well advised to sort out your family's preferences of the day *before* you start queueing. Who wants a starter, and what sort? Does everybody want a cooked meal, or does someone feel like a slice of ham and salad? (Note that meats and salads are usually presented separately). Are the children prepared to experiment, or will they just settle for *steak/frites*? The daily selection of hot dishes and their prices is usually written up on the wall behind the counter; try to sort it out while you are shuffling along in the queue.

The progression of food along the counter is fairly logical: first come the starters and cold food in general, then come desserts, then hot dishes, served to order through a hatch from the kitchen or from large containers (which means that you may not be able to see the food before you order it unless you watch very attentively what the people in front of you are served), and last come the drinks. Wines sometimes comes in small carafes, other drinks like beer, mineral water, apple juice and other fruit juices come in small bottles, which are opened at the check-out.

There are some endearing features about many French self-service restaurants. One is the microwave oven, placed centrally, where you can re-heat your meal if it has got cold by the time you reach your table; another is the water fountain for those who want a free drink of (iced) water. High-chairs are always provided.

Eating in a French self-service restaurant can be an enjoyable affair, especially with children, and it can be very much cheaper than being waited upon. The danger is that one is always tempted to take too much when confronted with a visual choice and ends up with a trayful of food which no-one can finish. Remember to go easy on the starters, they can be very filling. One is usually enough for two people if it is followed by a hot course. Three courses might cost you between 30F and 40F, which compares favourably with 45F to 60F for the same food in a conventional restaurant. Last summer the four of us had a very satisfactory lunch in C & A's self-service in Clermont-Ferrand for all of 85F, which included two courses for everyone, soft drinks for the children and wine for the grown-ups!

Conventional Restaurants

Restaurants in France come in all shapes and sizes, from the modest village restaurant in a room next to the bar or the unpretentious *brasserie* in the market square of a small town, to the palaces of haute cuisine, such as the renowned establishment of the Frères Troisgros at Roanne. Here the cheapest menu (in 1983) was a mere 220F plus 15% service! The pretentiousness or otherwise of a restaurant is not, in itself, a criterion of quality. You could enjoy some superb local cooking at a small brasserie or be served indifferent and unimaginative 'international' cuisines in the dazzling dining room of a big hotel.

Choosing a good place to eat is partly a matter of experience acquired during years of using one's eyes and one's nose in the service of one's stomach, and partly a matter of knowing on whom to rely for recommendations. Of the various Good Food Guides to France the red Michelin guide (around £6 from UK bookshops) and the Guide Gault-Millau (also about £6 from larger UK bookshops, or bought in France) are the most comprehensive. Of these two (both in French), the Michelin guide is the more generally useful, because it contains so much other information besides (see p.13). It must be remembered, though, that Michelin's recommendations of hotels and restaurants, except where they are starred, or marked with a red R (indicating 'a high standard of cooking at a moderate price') are not for food but for comfort and amenities! If price is an object, there are some 240 red-R restaurants listed in the Guide Michelin. After that, it's up, up to the stars! Michelin is (nearly) always reliable, and even a hotel or restaurant listed purely for its comfort and general standards is not likely to serve unacceptable food.

Guides are, of course, selective, and there are hundreds of restaurants all over the country which are not mentioned (or not *yet*) for good food but where one can eat a very satisfying or even an exceptionally good meal. Where the guides leave off, the individual detective work starts!

The presence of plenty of French customers in a restaurant used to be regarded as a sure sign of good food, but this can no longer be taken as an infallible rule. The French have always had a great predeliction for eating out, but in recent years, with generally increasing affluence and especially the demand for more leisure, the number of 'eater-outers' has considerably increased, and so, inevitably, has the number of undiscerning eaters.

Nearly all restaurants display their menus prominently outside the door — in fact they are required by law to do so. If there is no menu outside, the restaurant is either closed, or madame is still writing the menu out, or traffic is so sparse that the proprietor cannot afford the paper the menu is written on! Do not, under any circumstances, be talked into sitting down at a table by a bustling madame who is feverishly re-arranging the cutlery while she is reeling off a string of tempting dishes of the day — with no mention of a price anywhere. Be firm, stand by the door and demand to see the written menu, and if you don't like it, walk out a free man.

Menus usually contain clues as to the chef's attitude and the likely standard of food to be expected. Sheets of printed, yellowed card which have obviously been hanging in the display case for months, advertising a standard selection unrelieved by a choice of *plats du jour*, which change daily, does not augur well. Nor does a menu which contains nothing more imaginative that *crudités*, *côte de porc*, *steak*, *cotelette de veau*, which demand very little of the cook. Unpretentious food, if deliberately chosen for its cheapness, is one thing: indifferent food sold at a high price under the guise of respectability is something to steer clear of. In restaurants which have a bar attached or tables on the pavement, one can get an idea of the standard of food served by just ordering a pre-lunch or pre-dinner drink, in the middle of which one gets up to go to the toilets. With any luck, the way there leads through or past the restaurant or past the kitchen, where one can catch a glimpse of the food served and of the appearance of the kitchen; take a look at the same time at the cheese board, the fruit basket and catch a whiff of the cooking smells.

Larger restaurants offer an *à la carte* choice as well as three or four set menus; small restaurants in the country, which often concentrate on French Sunday trade, may just offer three set menus at different prices. Many restaurants offer a *menu touristique* or *menu conventionné* or *menu promotionel*. These are always the cheapest and usually inclusive of service (*service compris*), sometimes even inclusive of drink (*boisson comprise*). The *menu promotionel*, as the name implies, is an attempt on the part of the *patron* to promote custom, which logically implies that it is not only attractive but reasonably priced. These cheaper menus usually consist of three courses: starter, main course, and cheese or dessert. The *menu touristique* tends to look very much the same wherever one goes, undoubtedly reflecting popular taste: melon, or soup, or mixed salad (*crudités*), followed by steak and chips or chicken and chips, finishing with either cheese or one of the less complicated sweets like fruit tart, ice cream or yoghurt. Since the average price of such a menu is only around 40F or so one does not feel robbed.

At the other end of the scale is the *menu gastronomique*, which not only features more courses but far more interesting dishes and a choice of three or four items for each course as well. The *menu gastronomique* is meant to represent the very best efforts of the chef and often contains items which are not otherwise obtainable on the menu. But quality is accompanied by quantity, and unless you have an extremely healthy appetite and a lot of time to spare you should think twice before ordering it. Eating your way through five or six courses takes some doing. All the same, gastronomic need not mean astronomic. In a nice, middle-of-the-road restaurant untouched by international fame you can expect to pay 70-80F for such a menu. In a luxury establishment or one which is featured in a good food guide, you could pay twice or three times that.

For customers with a small capacity, and/or a smaller pocket there is at least one intermediate menu of four or five courses, starter, entrée, main course, sweet and cheese. If there are two such menus, the cheaper of the two is often very much the same as the other except that it is short of the entrée. If a restaurant offers set menus as well as an *à la carte* choice, one is always tempted to compare the two alternatives for value, and one always finds that a menu represents a distinct saving compared to the cost of the items ordered *à la carte*. Some people seem to think that if you order *à la carte* you get a better piece of meat or a bigger portion, but we have never found this to be so. There are only two reasons why you should order *à la carte*: either because an item in the *carte* takes your fancy which is not to be found in any of the set menus (which is frequently the case), or because you simply would not know what to do with a whole menu.

Feeding children with a small appetite in a conventional

restaurant can be a problem, because very few French restaurants, as yet, offer a specific children's menu (*menu enfant*). The Novotel hotel chain is a laudable exception. There are one or two solutions to this: if there are two children, they can share one menu between them (if they can agree on one!) if you (or they) think they cannot cope with a three-course menu each. The management will usually look benignly upon such an arrangement, and may or may not charge a small sum for the extra place setting (*couvert*). If there is only one child, you could choose a generous, four-or five-course menu for yourself and let the child share it, asking for an extra *couvert*. The management may not be too enamoured of the idea of '*le enfant va manger avec moi*' but they will usually be gracious about it and certainly charge for the *couvert*. Alternatively, you can ask whether one of the main dishes in a menu can be served on its own, as *plat du jour*. Or, if there is a *carte*, you can choose something *à la carte*, which is frequently an expensive and wasteful way of dealing with a small appetite. If chips is all your child will eat, dispense with all formalities and ask outright whether you can have *steak/frites* for him or her or even *frites* by themselves! Which is not to say that you will always be lucky.

Brasseries

Brasseries and no-nonsense restaurants frequently offer a *plat du jour* at lunchtime, which is the main course 'of the day' and can be ordered on its own. It is usually very popular and a good thing to choose, but in small restaurants with a busy clientele it often goes very quickly and it pays to get there early. A *brasserie*, incidentally, means literally 'brewery', and it started out as just that, i.e. a pub, or beer saloon. Meanwhile it has turned itself into an inexpensive type of restaurant (where, of course, quite a bit of drinking is done as well), frequented by people who want a snack or an uncomplicated meal in uncomplicated surroundings and not spend much time over it.*

---

*Paris restaurants are outside the general pattern of things. Most of them offer an *à la carte* selection only (no fixed-price menus) and many of them do not include service in their prices.-

In Paris and some other large French towns you will find that some of the better *Brasseries* have become large and expensive restaurants with the passage of time.

Le Relais Routiers

The Relais Routiers restaurant chain has firm adherents among foreign visitors to France. Literally, the term means something like 'road pull-in' or 'Highway café', but these modest restaurants must not be likened in standards to our 'transport cafés'. They are situated on or near main highways and are favoured by commercial drivers and lorry drivers, who, by and large, are good trenchermen and know value in food. There are some 3,500 of these establishments in France, recognizable by the red-and-blue plaque outside, and every year some 400 get weeded out to be replaced by new ones. Obviously, the inspection is keen. The criteria, which restaurants affiliated to *Les Routiers* must meet are: warm welcome, plentiful, good food and reasonable prices. The annual *Guide des Relais Routiers*, which lists them all, can be bought in the UK from motoring organisations and bookshops for around £5.

Le Café/Bar

Cafés are an essential part of the French social scene, for it is in such places that the fate of the nation is discussed and Frenchmen meet friends over a glass of something. In Paris and other cosmopolitan towns and seaside resorts women will do the same over coffee, icecream (or, indeed, over a 'glass of something'), sitting on the pavement terrace and watching the world go by, but the small, usually glum, all-indoor village cafe/bar with a few wooden tables and scruffy chairs on a bare floor does not witness many female customers. The women are, presumably, at home cooking the dinner. Nor does it see many foreign visitors, the reason being that it is just not a terribly attractive place to be spending one's money in. The pavement *café*, on the other hand, especially on a hot afternoon, is an admirable place for killing an hour over a cold drink. It must be added, though, that doing this with children, who can consume gallons of liquid, can be a very expensive exercise compared to getting a few litre-bottles of orangeade and apple juice from the supermarket!

Cafés are obliged to display a *table de consommation*, i.e. a price list of drinks where the customer can see it, which is usually behind the bar (*not* outside on the pavement!) and it is a good idea to go and take a look at it. It should indicate whether service is included (*Prix net* or *Service compris*) or whether it is additional to the price displayed (*Service non compris*)

Cafés are primarily places for consuming drink: alcoholic drink like wine by the glass, beer, *pastis* (aniseed-flavoured concentrate such as Pernod, Ricard, Anisette, which is mixed with water) and other aperitifs (abstain from Whisky, it is very expensive), as well as soft drinks and hot drinks like coffee, tea and chocolate. There is usually very little to be had to eat, perhaps a few *croissants* at breakfast time and *casse-croûtes* at all hours. Many *cafés* will let you consume your own sandwich, or cake, or whatever, on the premises.

Choosing a restaurant

How do you go about finding a place to eat in a large or medium-sized town? It is no good roaming the streets until everybody is famished. Go to the local *Syndicat d'Initiative* and ask for a list of restaurants *and* a town plan. Narrow your choice to a handful of restaurants of the type and category you have in mind, pin-point them on the town plan and go on an inspection tour. If you are travelling with a red Michelin guide or any other (good food) guide, do the same with their recommendations. Official restaurant lists published by tourist boards frequently do not give price indications. The Michelin guide has the advantage of giving information on minimum and maximum prices for fixed menus and à la carte meals, on whether service is included, or wine etc. is included too, and whether the restaurant serves modestly-priced wine by the carafe. *Boisson comprise* does not happen very often these days, but where it does, the customer is usually given a choice between a small carafe of vin ordinaire, a small bottle of mineral water, beer or a soft drink. Except in the case of fixed price menus there is no obligation on the part of the restauranteur to include service in his prices, but it is nowadays fairly normal for most hotels and restaurants (except the most precious) to do so. Where this is not the case, there will be a note on the menu: '*Service non compris*', in which case you will be expected to leave at least 15%.

Wine by the carafe, incidentally, *can* be very acceptable, especially in wine-growing areas, but it can just as easily be very disappointing. Rather than spoil a meal for the sake of a few francs one should go for a bottle of something reputable, or at least identifiable. After all, a good Bordeaux at 35-40F is a most acceptable price compared with prices in the UK. More is said about wines on pp.117-124.

Restaurant Opening Times

Opening times of restaurants of the conventional type (not self-service restaurants) are governed by the French habit of having quite a long lunch break, starting at 12 noon and finishing around 2.30 p.m., and then eating rather later in the evening than we do. In very popular holiday resorts, the rules tend to be more flexible and by the sea one is likely to find any number of seafront restaurants serving quick meals of the 'frites-with-everything' variety at most hours of the day, but elsewhere you are expected to tighten your belt and bear it until 8 p.m. This is hard luck on smaller children, who are used to eating at say 6 o'clock.

Snacks - and how to feed the children

Our idea of a 'snack' meal is alien to the French. But things are improving! There is now a *hypermarché* or two on the outskirts of every decent-size town, whose cafeteria re-opens around 6.30 p.m. (it is likely to be closed from 2.30 till 6.30 p.m.), and there is very often a self-service restaurant *in* the town which starts to serve meals earlier than 8 p.m.

In popular resorts some self-service restaurants serve meals all day. If you are lucky you may be near a *Courte-Paille* grill restaurant (see p.61) of which there are some 75 all over France, mostly outside larger towns, just off motorways and main roads. The number is increasing annually. These distinctive, round, whitewashed little places with thatched roofs open from breakfast till late at night, serving grilled food with chips and dressed salad in very pleasant, rustic surroundings. Pork chops, steaks, chicken portions and sausages are cooked before your eyes over a glowing wood fire in a big brick fireplace, the usual selection of drinks is available and afterwards there is something simple like tart or icecream, served in an attractive way for children. One cannot say that *Courtes-Pailles* are especially cheap, nor are they particularly expensive (entrecote steak, garnished, around 40F). What they serve is not haute cuisine, but it is good food, nicely and quickly served in civilized surroundings.

Restaurants like *crêperies* which serve gap-filler meals, are to be found in increasing numbers. A *crêperie* visited in Caen recently had a really impressive selection on its menu. There were 15 varieties of *crêpe*, all sweet, of course, from a *crêpe* nature at 4.00F to a *Crêpe Malba* at 11.00F. In addition there were no less than 18 *galettes* with savoury fillings, from an *galette oeuf* for 6.50F to a *galette aux poireaux jambon Gruyère* for 12.50F. All these filled pancakes were made with delicious wholemeal flour and made an excellent small meal. Two made a substantial main course in most cases. The same *crêperie* (*Crêperie du Petit chef*) could also provide a choice of 9 omelettes with various fillings, eight sweets and a fair selection of drinks including cider and *vin de table.*

Cafés and *brasseries* often display a sign in their window which says '*Casse-croûte*' and this, believe it or not, means snack, or quick-lunch, and can be anything from a sandwhich or a *Croque Monsieur* (toasted cheese and ham sandwich) to *oeufs sur le plat* (fried eggs) or sausages and chips. *Casse-croûtes* are really meant to be served at normal mealtimes, but you can always go into a *brasserie* at 6 o'clock and ask 'Est-ce-que vous servez les casse-croûtes maintenant?' (do you serve snacks now?), and you may be lucky. Out in the country, if everything else fails and people simply cannot wait till 8 o'clock, the solution is a picnic meal, and that, in France (see section on SHOPS AND SHOPPING, p.102) is really no problem.

Fermé (Closed)

When you see this sign outside a restaurant, you know that you have failed to consult your red Michelin guide, which gives weekly closing days as well as annual holiday periods of restaurants and hotels it recommends. There is no fixed rule about the day of the week on which a restaurant is likely to be closed, but *lundi* (that Monday again) and *mardi* (Tuesday) are by far the commonest. Many restaurants, especially in towns, close all day Sunday, or at least on Sunday evening. Restaurants in the country are more likely to be open for lunch on Sunday, because they cater for the French enthusiasm for getting out of towns on a Sunday and having lunch in the country.

From the middle of July until the end of August France goes on holiday. It is, therefore, reasonable to expect to find restaurants in larger towns, which draw on a largely local clientele, to be closed for some or all of that time. Going to a large town (including Paris) in August in search of a gastronomic experience is unlikely to be very rewarding because the choice will be severely restricted. Restaurants in major holiday centres, which rely on holiday traffic, close instead in the off-season.

A Question of Breakfast

Unless you and your family are avid breakfast eaters and can devour chunks of French bread with butter and pre-packed jam, hotel breakfasts at 12F or more are often a waste of time and money.

Some hotels do go so far as to serve *croissants*, but further than that the gastronomic pleasures of French breakfast do not extend. No boiled eggs, ham or cheese unless you specifically ask for them, and pay for them. For casual breakfast eaters, and children in particular tend to fall into this category, it is much more convenient and much less boring to have a hot drink at a *café/bar* after having checked out of the hotel. This has the added advantage of being cheaper and enabling you to buy your own *croissants* or pastries. Occasionally a cafe will have *croissants* on the counter at breakfast time, but more often than not the proprietor will indicate the *boulangerie* across the road and tell you to get your own.

If you have some food shopping to do for the day and you happen to spot a *hypermarché* you might do worse than have breakfast at the cafeteria there. Unfortunately, there is no universal rule on cafeteria opening hours; some open when the shops do, other not until 10 a.m. and on Monday morning they are probably closed altogether. There is one more thing you should do while having breakfast at a *hypermarché*: fill the car up with petrol. Petrol is always cheaper at hypermarkets.

One particular variety of hotel breakfast which we have come across in recent years does deserve special mention, and that is the breakfast buffet. This can be a thoroughly enjoyable affair if you are not in a great hurry to get away. Children enjoy the novelty of it and the choice of things they would not normally be offered for breakfast. In recent years the Novotel hotel chain, in a promotional effort to attract families, offered a rather splendid deal to children under 15 by which they were not only accommodated totally free of charge in their parent's room, but could indulge in the buffet breakfast at half price! Normally, of course, a buffet breakfast might be between 50% and 100% more expensive than a simple French breakfast, but if you 'can do it justice' it is extremely good value, because it will keep you going well into the afternoon. You can help yourself to a selection of food set out on a large table, and you can eat as much of anything as you like. There may be several different types of bread, rolls, *croissants*, *brioches*, butter, jam, honey, eggs (which you boil yourself), ham, sausage, hard cheese, cheese spread, cottage cheese, yoghurt, fruit juice and a basket of fresh fruit. Hot beverages are normally served at the table and are of the usual variety: *café au lait* (white coffee), *café crême* (black coffe with evaporated milk served separately), *chocolat* (hot chocolate) or *thé citron* (lemon tea). The type of tea used in France does not lend itself to making a nice, strong cup of English milk tea.

The language of the Menu — a few common terms explained

Styles of cooking meat, poultry, fish:

maison according to the recipe of the house (usually simple)
chasseur with mushrooms, flavoured with shallots and white wine
jardinière with vegetables
vert pré grilled meat served with straw potatotes, watercress and *maitre d'hotel* butter
bonne femme according to the recipe of the proprietoress, homely, simple
à la boulangère cooked in a fireproof dish in the oven
à la bourguignonne with a red-wine sauce and garnished with mushrooms, small onions and strips of bacon
à la dieppoise fish cooked in white wine, garnished with mussels and crayfish tails
à la financìere garnished with a *ragôut* of cock's kidney, sweet-breads, mushrooms, olives and strips of truffles
à la forestìere garnished with chopped mushrooms, streaky bacon and diced potatoes fried in butter
au gratin browned under the grill, usually with cheese on top

à la languedocienne garnished with tomatoes, aubergines, boletus mushrooms and garlic flavoured sauce
à la lìegoise poultry cooked with juniper berries
à la maconnaise meat dishes flavoured with red wine
meunière coated with flour and fried in butter; applies to fish, e.g. sole and trout
à la Nantua garnished with crayfish tails or crayfish purée
à la niçoise cooked with tomatoes and flavoured with garlic
à la paysanne cooked with streaky bacon, carrots, turnips, onion and celery
à la printanière garnished with early or mixed vegetables
à la Provençale cooked with tomatoes and garlic, or garlic alone

Some food items which appear widely in restaurant menus, especially modestly priced ones:

Crudités mixed salad served as hors d'oeuvre
Jambon cru raw, smoked ham
Jambon de Paris cooked ham
Saucisse sec or *saucisse de montagne* slices of air-dried pork similar to coarse salami
Terrine coarse meat or game pâté, often home-made
Rillettes a coarse but spreadable paste made from crushed pork (and goose meat)
Coquilles St. Jacques scallops served in their shells with a cream sauce, *au gratin*
Escargots maison snails served with garlic butter either in shells or little porcelain pots
Charcuterie assortie various cold sliced meats and sausages
Fruits de mer a selection of shellfish
Tomates vinaigrettes sliced tomato dressed with onion, oil and vinegar
Oeufs farcis hard-boiled eggs stuffed with any kind of filling
Oeufs mayonnaise hard-boiled eggs dressed with mayonnaise
Quenelles dumplings made of a forcemeat of all kinds of meat, poultry, fish or game
Tournedos a thick-cut round of fillet steak, either plainly fried or grilled or garnished in one of many ways: the best cut of beef
Médaillon strictly speaking the same as Tournedos, but also

applied to small, round cuts of other meats i.e. pork, veal or poultry — if in doubt, ask

Noisette the same applies as to Médaillon, but most frequently used for lamb

Entrecôte, contre-filet, faux filet, châteaubriand all cuts of beef steak (see La boucherie, p.000)

Côte de pork, de veau, d'agneau pork, veal and lamb chop respectively

Brochette de . . . cubed meat on skewers. Often served on rice

Rôti de porc, de veau roast pork and veal respectively, usually served with a tasty sauce

Gigot d'agneau roast or braised leg of lamb

Lapin chasseur rabbit stew with mushrooms

Poulet rôti roast chicken

Coq an vin casseroled chicken prepared with streaky bacon, mushrooms, herbs and red wine. (Some recipes include the blood of the chicken)

Dinde or *dindonneau* young turkey

Caneton duckling

Cailles quail. Very popular and served grilled, roasted or braised in a variety of casserole dishes

Pintadeau young guinea fowl. Also very popular and prepared in ways similar to quail or partridge

Perdrix, perdreau partridge. There are quite a lot of these about during the shooting season

Cassoulet an inexpensive but tasty and filling dish originating in the Languedoc: haricot bean stew with pieces of salt pork or bacon, mutton, goose or duck, and garlic sausage

Gras-double tripe, cooked in a variety of ways

Ris de veau calf's sweetbreads, usually braised, in a sauce, or sautéed in butter

*Pommes (de terre) rissolées** raw or boiled potatoes, diced or sliced and fried in butter in the pan

Pommes (de terre) vapeur steamed potatoes

Pommes (de terre) sautées same as *pommes rissolées*

---

*Strictly speaking, *pommes de terre* are potatoes, and *pommes* are apples. It is, however, customary to drop *de terre* for simplicity's sake where it is obvious that potatoes are meant.

Pommes (frites) allumettes —very finely sliced chips
(*Pommes*) *croquettes* shapes of potato purée rolled in bread-crumbs and deep-fried
Purée (de pommes de terre) mashed potato, made with butter and milk: sometimes referred to as *pommes mousseline*, although, strictly speaking, that is something a bit more elaborate
Ratatouille a mixture of aubergines, courgettes, onions, tomatoes, peppers and garlic braised in olive oil
Fromage blanc cream cheese, eaten with sugar as a dessert
Tarte maison fruit flan made to the recipe of the house, home-made
Crêpes pancakes, usually rolled up around a fruit filling
Compote de . . . stewed fruit, served cold, e.g. *compote d'abricot*
Ananas au kirsch a slice or two of pineapple sprinkled with kirsch, with maybe a cherry in the middle
Glace ice cream

11. FINANCE

French banks open five days a week, but for some the fifth day is Saturday. All branches of *Crédit Agricole*, France's most widespread popular bank, open at normal hours on a Saturday and close, instead, on a Monday. Opening hours for banks vary by region, but broadly speaking they open from 8.30 to 12.00 in the mornings and from 3 p.m. to 5.30 p.m. in the afternoons. The best thing you can do is to check locally on the opening hours so that you will not be caught out. To cut out any risk of this happening we make a point of providing ourselves with adequate funds to take us through from Friday to Tuesday. Some hotels will change money, though the rate of exchange will not be as good as that given by a bank. This is natural, since the hotel has to take its foreign currency along to a bank and exchange it there. Other than at banks and hotels, money can usually be changed at international airports and at border crossings which are in frequent use. In both cases the rates will differ little from the normal bank rates.

To avoid carrying large amounts of currency or traveller's cheques you can arrange for money to be transferred to a bank abroad. This requires knowing the name and location of a particular bank, but is very useful if you are staying in one place for any length of time.

Eurocheque is a useful means of acquiring funds at banks which display the sign. You need to get the requisite Eurocheque card at your local bank in the UK. When presenting this to any bank in France (or elsewhere in Europe) which belongs to the system, your normal cheques will be honoured. Normally, you will be restricted to £50 per cheque per day.

If you run out of money but have adequate funds in your own bank at home you can simply contact your bank and request that funds be transferred to a named bank in France for payment to you. All that is necessary is a telephone call to your bank requesting the transfer (which will be made in francs), but this must be followed by confirmation by way of a telegram or letter. The transfer will take two or three days and the French bank will be instructed to pay the money to you on presentation of suitable identification.

Credit cards

As in most countries today a great deal of expenditure can be taken care of with the help of credit cards. American Express, Carte Bleue (Visa), Diners Clubs and Eurocard are widely accepted for petrol, hotel bills, meals in restaurants and in quite a number of shops. At the worst you will be called upon to produce means of identity (passport) but, in our experience, little or no attention is paid to this. The rate of exchange used in dealing with payments made in this way appears favourable and since many of your expenditures may not appear on your account for nearly two months, this is an excellent way of getting along without large amounts of cash or travellers cheques. Be careful to ask if a particular credit card is actually accepted before making the purchase.

12. DEALING WITH ILLNESS

The worst that can happen on holiday is that one of you falls seriously ill. In 22 years of travelling the Continent this never happened to us until, one day in 1980, safely ensconced in a *gîte* some 30 km from Cahors, in the open country with the nearest house some 3 or 4 km away, my wife woke up at 6 a.m. complaining of unusually bad stomach ache. After 30 minutes this had developed to the point where she became quite desperate. I rapidly dressed the children, at the same time trying to think where the nearest doctor might be. Then I remembered that we had passed the Centre Hospitalier in Cahors on a previous evening. It would be easy to find but was over 30 km on very windy and narrow roads.

I finally drew up in the entrance gate to the hospital at 7.25 a.m. and grabbed the first two figures I could see in white coats. 'Ma femme est très malade' I said prosaicly, and within seconds a porter appeared, whisked her from the car, into the lift and up to the emergency ward. There, in a state, by now, of semi-consciousness, she was examined immediately by the staff on duty, and the *interniste* (specialist for internal complaints) was sent for. She was subjected to lengthy X-rays and ultra-sound scanning before being removed to the intensive care unit and given treatment. In the meantime, I was not asked to complete any forms nor given anything but reassurance from the house surgeon. To cut a long story short, the condition was eventually diagnosed as 'probable' chemical poisoning (through eating unwashed grapes from a vineyard!) and my wife left the hospital three days later, very groggy but otherwise better.

We cannot speak too highly of the efficiency and speed with which the French hospital acted and of their friendly, confidence-inspiring attitude.

CONCLUSIONS: in case of serious illness or accident make for a hospital if there is one within easy reach and report to the outpatients department. If you cannot cope with the transport, telephone the nearest hospital and ask for assistance. They can arrange for an ambulance. It is clear that in a somewhat serious case like ours, gettting a local doctor involved could only have led to delay with possible serious results. We have heard of many cases of illness by travellers who have taken the commonsense approach and simply reported to a hospital outpatients department, where they have always been well received. During her stay in Cahors hospital my wife was gleefuly descended upon by the staff nurse bringing along an English family with a language problem. Would she tell them that their small son, who had a nasty septic wound on his foot, had to be left behind overnight for treatment etc. etc. Being on their way home from a holiday in the 'Med' this family was highly relieved to find a sympathetic hospital doctor taking care of a situation which, since they were on the road, was becoming a real worry.

It goes without saying that with a not-so-urgent common or garden ailment like stomach upset, flue or cystitis you should see a doctor, not a hospital. For minor ailments such as a sore throat (*mal de gorge*), tonsillitis (*angine*) a cold (*un rhume*) or a headache (*mal à la tête*), the chemist (*la pharmacie*) can be relied upon to recommend an effective remedy. Medicines obtained from a chemist without a doctor's prescription will not, of course, be reimbursed by any health insurance.

Doctors are thick on the ground in France and many are specialists, e.g. for internal ailments, nose and ear conditions, children's complaints. The plaque outside the surgery, which is most likey to be in his private house, will state what type of specialist a doctor is, if any, and also indicate the consulting hours. You can ask the local tourist office for a list of doctors (or at least the address and telephone number of one doctor) at the very beginning of your stay somewhere. In practice, most people leave this sort of thing to chance and, when the need arises, enlist the help of the hotel receptionist, the *gîte* proprietor or the campsite warden. A French doctor, incidentally, is just as prepared to come out on a house call as his English counterpart and will probably come more quickly, because he is less likely to be overworked.

Doctors do, of course, expect immediate payment. Whether you are privately insured or hold a National Health form E111 you must, without fail, ask the doctor for a formal receipt. Also ask him to give you a form called a *feuille de maladie* or *feuille de soins*. This is essential if you want to claim under the reciprocal Common Market health arrangements (form E111). If the doctor prescribes any medicine, which you buy at the *pharmacie* at an astronomic price, the chemist will enter these on the *feuille*. The medicine box or bottle will have a price sticker on it, which you take off and stick on the form also. Possibly the chemist might do this himself. In addition, you must ask him for the prescription back. If you are privately insured and do not intend to make use of an E111 all you have to ask the chemist for is the prescription and the receipt. Any further visits to the doctor or chemist will be entered in the *feuille* in the same way, and at the end of your treatment you take all your bits of paper, not forgetting form E111, to the local *caisse primaire d'assurance maladie* (address from doctor, chemist or telephone directory) who, depending on how busy they are, will take anything between half-an-hour and half a day completing the formalities. Do not expect to get any money back then and there. A refund of up to 75% of your medical expenses will be made to your home address. The same goes for dental treatment and outpatients treatment at hospitals. In the case of in-hospital treatment the hospital will recover a percentage of the cost directly from the *caisse primaire* if you show them your form E111. If the hospital is not a public but a private hospital you may be asked to pay the whole bill yourself and recover a percentage from the *caisse primaire*, as above. Further instructions about the whole procedure are contained in the DHSS leaflet SA36, which is issued together with Form E111. To obtain a form E111, to which every UK resident (and his dependents) is entitled, who is currently paying, or has ever paid, national insurance contributions, whether he is employed, self-employed or unemployed, apply to your local Department of Health and Social Security.

Like most things in life, Form E111 has its shortcomings. It provides for a partial refund of medical expenses only, and it does not cover treatment by non-panel doctors and private, non-approved hospitals. A private health insurance, on the other hand, does not normally cover so-called 'pre-existing' conditions or illness arising from manual work or certain sports activities, but apart from that it guarantees a full refund of just about all medical expenses up to a very high maximum including, in some policies, additional travelling expenses, nursing care en route, etc. It follows that the wise thing to do is to go for belt and braces and take a form E111 as well as a private insurance, so that one will cover what the other does not. The best type of insurance is a comprehensive holiday insurance of the kind offered by the motoring organisations, ferry companies and travel agents, which, apart form medical expenses, covers for cancellation, personal liability, death, loss of luggage and money. Having to pay a premium of, say, £40 for three weeks for four persons may seem a lot at the time, but when you consider that one day in a French hospital may cost you £100, (approx. Fr. 1000) having to pay even a proportion of a prolonged hospital stay appears far less attractive.

As a tailpiece, it might be as well to explain what situation would have arisen if our children had had to return to the UK on their own. Since neither had a passport of their own, it would have been necessary to make special arrangements at a British Consulate when they departed. In a similar situation, if you do not know the address or telephone number of the nearest consul, you should visit the local civil police, who will help solve the problem.

A few useful phrases

Il me faut un docteur	I need a doctor
une ambulance	an ambulance
Je suis malade	I am ill
Mon enfant (ma femme) est malade	My child (my wife) is ill
J'ai mal ici . . .	I have a pain here . . .
J'ai mal à la tête	I have a headache
mal de gorge	a sore throat
de la temperature	a high temperature
un rhume	a cold
un toux	a cough
un abcès	an abcess
la diarrhé	diarrhoea
un coup de chaleur	a heatstroke
J'ai envie de vomiter	I want to be sick
J'ai une assurance maladie	I have a health insurance

13. LE PTT FRANÇAIS

'PTT' stands for '*Postes, Télégraphes et Téléphones*', and means, of course the French Post Office. You find one wherever you see this sign, which is a blue, stylized bird on a white background. Post boxes, on the other hand, are yellow, so are PTT vans. A collection from a post box, by the way, is *une levée. The opening hours* of post offices are normally 8 a.m. to 7 p.m. (possibly closed for two hours during lunch in small towns and villages) Monday to Friday and from 8 a.m. to 12 noon on Saturdays. Most main post offices in large towns also open on Sunday morning. French PTT's perform exactly the same functions as their counterparts in the UK. You are most likely to want to go into a post office either to buy stamps, or to make a telephone call (see p.151) or to collect poste restante mail.

Stamps are best bought at *le tabac* (short for *bureau de tabac*), which is the Newsagent-cum-tobacconist, usually recognizable by what is supposed to be a large red cigar-sign (often illuminated after dark) hanging outside his shop. In large towns, where the post office may be half an hour's walk away and sport long queues at every counter, this is a more convenient way of getting those few bits of sticky paper for the postcards you have just written. However, it is not safe to assume that the man or lady in the *tabac* is *au fait* with postal rates to foreign countries, and it is, therefore, a good idea to pick up a leaflet on postal charges (*taxes postales*) at the first post office you get to in France. This will list, apart from telephone and telegram charges, rates for letters (*lettres*), postcards (*cartes postales*), printed matter (*imprimés*), small packets (*petits paquets*). If you are thinking of sending a present home to auntie, who is looking after the dog, choose something which weighs no more than 1 kg when wrapped. You can then send it as *petit paquet*, which needs only a green customs sticker. If the present weighs more than 1 kg you will have to send it as *paquet-poste*, which starts to become expensive and involves form filling.

Poste restante mail can be addressed to you at any post office. When giving your friends your address in France, make sure you include the five-figure code which precedes the name of the town or village, e.g.

Mr John Smith
Poste restante
74000 Annecy
France

In a larger town, which has more than one post office, *poste restante* mail is always sent to the main post office. Don't forget to take your passport along when collecting *poste restante* mail. You will be asked to show your *pièce d'identité* (passport, usually) and you will be charged per item of mail you collect (2F in 1983).

Mail, whether to a private address or *poste restante*, can be redirected. This service of *réexpédition* is quite expensive (upwards of 45F in 1983), so you don't want to make a habit of having your mail sent after you every few days.

Ordinary telegrams are quite reasonable. A ten-words-maximum telegram inside France or a minimum-charge telegram (7 words) to the UK cost under 20F in 1983.

Useful phrases

Where is the main post office in this town?	*Où est le bureau principal des PTT de cette ville?*
I would like . . . stamps at . . . francs	*Je voudrais . . . timbres-postes à . . . francs*
Where is the poste restante counter?	*Où est le guichet de la poste restante?*
How much is the letter?	*Combien coûte cette lettre?*

I would like to have my mail forwarded	*Je voudrais faire réexpédier mon courrier*
I would like to send a telegram	*Je voudrais expédier un telegramme*

The *Ministère des PTT* publishes a multi-lingual booklet each year, which gives up-to-date information on services available. It also illustrates current coins and bank-notes and includes multi-lingual vocabulary and phraseology. It is available from the French Government Tourist Office in London (for address see p. 185), also from some post offices and tourist offices in the bigger towns of main tourist regions.

14. MAKING A TELEPHONE CALL

Not so many years ago, if you found yourself faced with the need to make a 'phone call from some small French village, you almost invariably had to resort to the hazardous procedure of going into the local café or bar, which had the only public telephone in the place. One could never be quite sure whether one was doing the right and proper thing, especially if there wasn't an official *Téléphone Public* sign in sight. Perhaps it had dropped off? or perhaps the other bar across the road was the correct one to go to? Once you had plucked up courage to go inside you had to decide whether you were following the rules by politely asking the man behind the bar: 'May I use your telephone?', or whether it was the done thing to boldly walk across to where it was hanging on the wall and grab it, only to find that it was one of those that did not take coins and you had to ask the bar-keeper for a *jeton* (token).

One hectic summer afternoon somewhere north of Limoges, deciding that we were running too late to chance getting a bed for the night without making a telephone reservation, we staggered into a very dismal-looking and empty bar by the road and, after having made the call from a coin operated telephone, were just about to stagger out again, waving politely, when the proprietor behind the bar straightened himself out, gave us a withering look and bawled threateningly: 'Shouldn't one be drinking something?' or the French equivalent thereof. Then followed an arm-waving tirade about people's manners, and what was the world coming to, by the end of which we were sitting red-faced and chastened in front of two cups of coffee and two Cokes, which delighted the children but didn't help our timetable.

One is much less likely to have this kind of embarrassing experience nowadays, because the PTT have made tremendous progress in installing shining aluminium and glass telephone booths in even the humblest of villages. They are nearly always in a prominent position, in a square, or outside the church, and you can hardly miss them. In towns, of course, especially in the centre, you will find a telephone round every other corner, and there is always one in or outside a post office and in or outside a railway station.

French public telephones at the time of writing take 50 centimes, 1 Franc and 5 Franc pieces. 50 centimes is only useful for local calls. Up until recently, except in some of the larger cities, 50 centimes bought a local call of unlimited duration. By the end of 1984, however, it will buy only the first 3 minutes, the next 6 minutes, being charged at 1F and any subsequent 6 minutes thereafter at 70 centimes. For trunk calls, the unit charge (in 1983) is 60 centimes, and depending on the distance, you get 120, 72, or 45 seconds (up to 100 km) or 11 seconds (over 100 km) per unit. Person-to-person and reverse-charge calls inside France incur a surcharge (8.60F in 1983). The current rates, together with dialling codes for countries abroad and instructions on how to use the telephone (in three languages) are displayed in every booth. It is safer not to rely on the displayed rates, though, since they may be out of date. Inflation is not unknown in France, and postal rates increase from time to time.

The procedure is simple and similar to that found in most modern booths in the UK.

Lift receiver
Insert money
If your coins do not show up in the display window, press black button at top for return of coins and try again.
Wait for continuous tone
Dial
When subscriber answers, talk. There is no button to press!
Insert more money as you see your coins disappearing in the display window.

How to dial a number in the same town or départément
Simply dial the number without any prefix.

How to dial a number in another French département

1. First dial 16 to get an 'outside' line. You will hear a series of rapid bleeps.
2. When these have changed to a continuous tone, dial the code of the department, which is a two-digit number (except for

Paris, which is 1), for example, the code for Allier is 70, that for Dordogne 51, and that for Bas du Rhin 91. If you don't know the department code, you can find it in the red Michelin guide. It is the last item, preceeded by a little dial symbol, on the first line of any place entry.

If you cannot find an entry in the Michelin for the actual town or village you want to 'phone, look up any larger towns in the same *département* for which there is an entry and take the code from that.

If you are given a telephone number and it looks like this, for example:

Tel. (54) 78-06-70

the (54) is the departmental code, the department in this case being Loir-et-Cher. Unless you are already in Loir-et-Cher when you make the call, you have to prefix 54 by 16!

3. Dial the subscriber's number (in this case 780670).

Calls inside France are cheaper by 50% between 7.30 p.m. and 8 a.m. Monday to Friday, and between 2 p.m. on Saturday and 8 a.m. on Monday.

How to dial a number in the UK

1. Dial 19 to get a 'line out'. You will hear a series of rapid bleeps.
2. When these have changed to a continuous tone, continue by dialling the code for Great Britain (to be found under Grande Bretagne in the list displayed in the telephone booth), which is 44.
3. Follow this immediately by the STD-code in the UK, omitting the 0, i.e. if 0206 is the code for Colchester, you dial 206.
4. Follow this immediately by the subscriber's number in the UK. For example if you wanted to dial Colchester 76011 from France, the dialling sequence would be:

19 (pause) 44 — 206 — 76011

How to dial a number in other countries

The same procedure applies to other countries. Wherever the

STD town code is preceded by 0, omit the 0 when dialling from France. Country codes for some other European countries are:

Holland	19-31
Belgium	19-32
Germany	19-49
Switzerland	19-41
Austria	19-43
Spain	19-34
Ireland	19-353
Italy	19-39

Calls to Common Market countries (including UK) are cheaper by one-third between 9 p.m. and 8 a.m. Monday to Saturday and all day Sunday. At the peak rate, a 1-minute call to the UK costs about 4F (in 1983).

Calling the Operator (opératrice)

Insert 50 centimes. Dial 19-33 plus the code number of the *département* in which you are.

Useful phrases:

I cannot get through on my STD call to . . .	*Je n'arrive pas à obtenir ma communication en automatique pour . . .*
I have been cut off. Could you, please, re-connect me	*La communication a été coupée Auriez-vous l'obligeance de la rétablir?*
Hold the line please	*Ne quittez pas!*
You are through	*Vous êtes en communication*
I would like to telephone to . . .	*Je voudrais téléphoner à . . .*
Please give me the following number . . .	*Voulez-vous me demander le numéro suivant . . .*
There is no reply	*Le correspondant ne réspond pas*
I would like a person-to-person call to . . .	*Je voudrais un préavis pour . . .*
I would like a reversed-charge call to . . .	*Je voudrais une communication PCV à . . .*

Calling Directory Enquiries (renseignements)

Insert 50 centimes.

Dial 12. If you want a number in the UK, ask for *reuseignements internationaux – Grande Bretagne*

Useful phrases:

Could you find for me the number of the following subscriber (in UK)...	*Voulez-vous m'aviser le numéro du correspondant suivant (en Grande Bretagne...*

Making a call from a post office

If you cannot get hold of change for a public coin-operated telephone, if the number you want is not STD, if you want to look up a number or if you cannot get through and haven't the courage to tackle the operator; go to the post office and ask for help at the telephone counter.

Main post offices in larger towns stock a certain number of foreign telephone directories in addition to the directories of all the French *départements*.

Useful phrases:

Would you give me the telephone directory for . . .	*Voulez-vous me donner l'annuaire téléphonique de . . . ?*
I would like some coins, please	*Je voudrais de la monnaie*
How much is a call to . . . ?	*Quel est le prix d'une communication téléphonique pour . . . ?*
Which cabin . . . ?	*Quelle cabine . . . ?*

In larger post offices there will be several numbered cabins. You will be asked to go into one of them, pick up the receiver and wait to be connected. If you telephone from a hotel, restaurant, café etc. it will cost up to 40% more.

15. SIGHTSEEING

Cathedrals, Castles and Châteaux

The architecture of the great buildings of France has always been a great and rewarding attraction not only to serious students of the subject but to visitors and holidaymakers in general. There are hundreds of architectural gems strewn all over France, and one does not have to follow a purposeful itinerary to come across some of them. Nor is it always the large and famous buildings that leave a lasting impression. But since one has to start somewhere, we list here, what are, by common consent, the most outstanding cathedrals:

Albi, 1282 (Tarn)
Amiens, 1220 (Somme) Largest French cathedral
Beavais, 1247 (Oise) Highest vault in Europe, 48m
Bourges, 1195 (Cher)
Chartres, 1194 (Eure-et-Loir) First example of High Gothic
Coutances, 1066 (Manche)
Le Puy, 12th cent. (H.Loire)
Metz, 13th cent. (Moselle)
Reims, 1211 (Marne)
Rouen, 13th cent. (Seine-Maritime)
Strasbourg, 1230 (Bas-Rhin)

There are sixty or so more which merit star treatment in the red Michelin guide and, in addition, a number of outstanding churches which do not rate as cathedrals. Foremost among these, in our opinion, is the Romanesque pilgrimage church at Vezelay in Burgundy.

France is a country not only of churches and cathedrals but also of castles and châteaux. We use both terms here to differentiate between fortified castles used for defence and châteaux which were used as residences and country retreats. There are quite a number which served both purposes. Top of the list of châteaux,

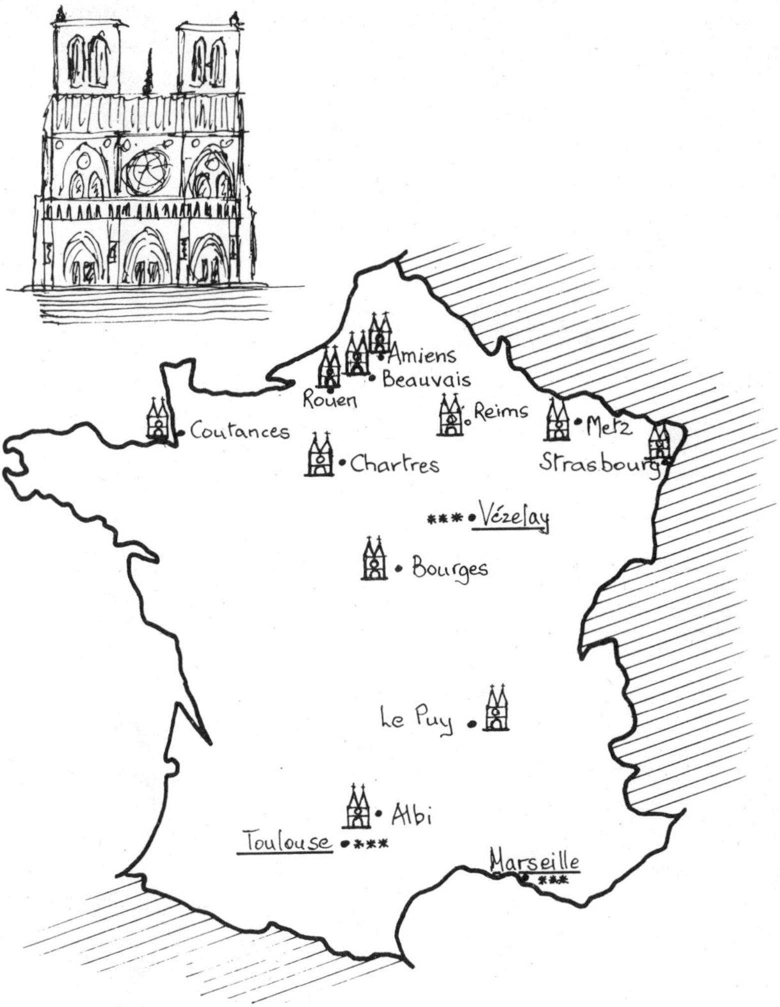

Eleven 3-star Cathedrals and three outstanding Basilicas

though commonly referred to as 'palace' is Versailles, one of the most copied buildings of France and one of the three great palaces of France, the other two being Fontainebleau, also near Paris, and Compiègne. some 80 km north of Paris in the *département* of Oise.

Brittany's major castles are fortresses, among the most important ones being Fourgères, Josselin and Vitré, and so are those of Normandy, where Falaise and the mighty ruins of Château-Gaillard, Richard Lionheart's castle, should be at the top of any itinerary.

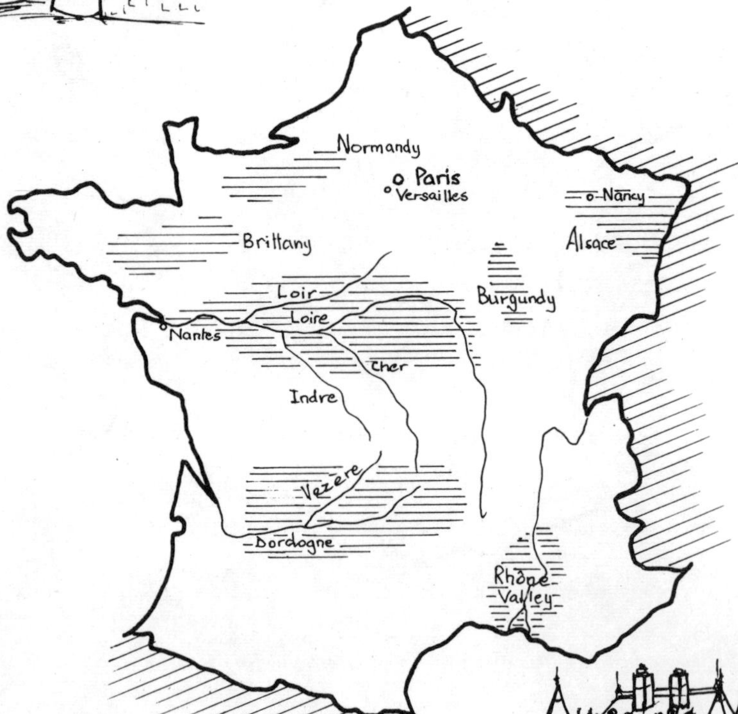

Main concentrations of Castles and Châteaux

In the region of Alsace-Vosges-Lorraine there are two castles worthy of a visit: the fortified castle of Le Haut Koenigsbourg in the Vosges mountains, and the old Ducal Palace in the historic town of Nancy. Burgundy has a number of attractive, small châteaux (nothing to do with wine), the best two being Bussy-Raboutin and Ancy-le-Franc, both north-west of Dijon. In the Dordogne there is a fortified castle or the ruins of one round every other corner. The ones not to be missed are Hautefort, Montal, Castlenau, Bonaguil (ruined) and the Château de Val, a picture book castle *par excellence*, spectacularly perched on a rocky outcrop above a dammed section of the Dordogne.

The classic region of fortified castles and *châteaux* is, of course, the Loire valley, i.e. the Loire and its tributaries. A complete list would comprise some 45, and to appreciate them all calls for a fair number of repeat visits to the area. The most outstanding ones, from west to east, starting with the Château Ducal at Nantes and the mighty fortress of Angers, are Serrent, Le Plessis-Bourré, Saumur, Chinon, Ussé, Azay-le-Rideau, Langeais, Loche, Chenonceaux, Amboise, Chaumont, Villandrey, Valençay, Cheverny, Blois and Chambord.

Caves and gorges

Among the natural wonders of France which are firmly-established tourist attractions are the many caves in the south and south-east of the country. These caves were formed in prehistoric times, perhaps as long as 30,000 years ago in many cases, due to the erosion of the limestone by rain and underwater streams. When discovered by modern man, many of these subterranean refuges of stone-age man were found to contain perfectly preserved paintings of animals, human figures and hunting scenes on their walls and ceilings. The best known of these prehistoric-art caves is the Grotto de Lascaux in Périgord which has now, alas, been closed to the public to avoid further irreparable damage to the painting caused by the constant stream of visitors. There are others which can still be viewed, at least at the time of writing: Bara-Bahau and Font de Gaume, south-west of the grotto of Lascaux and not far from Les Eyzies-de-Tayac, the 'capital of prehistory'; the cave of Rouffignac some 12 kilometres north of Les Eyzies; and the cave of Pech Merle, 33

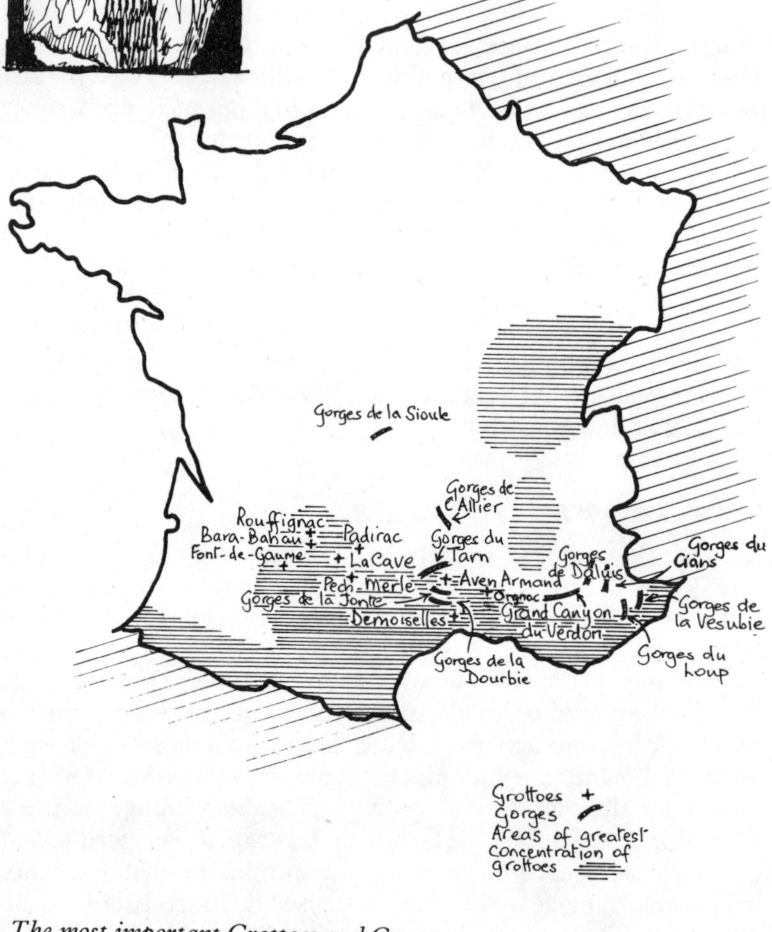

The most important Grottoes and Gorges

kilometres east of Cahors. Most of the French caves however, are famous not for their prehistoric remains but for their sheer size, their underground rivers, or their amazing stalagmites, stalagtites and other mineral formations. The largest and best-known are the Gouffre de Padirac (*gouffre* meaning pit, or abyss) on the edge of the Causse de Gramat near St. Céré in the Dordogne; Lacave, not far away to the east; the incredible *Aven Armand* in the Gorges du Tarn region; the equally impressive *Aven d'Orgnac* in the Ardèche region; and the Grotte des Demoiselles in Hérault. There are many more in these and other parts of France. A leaflet containing a map and a list of caves with their opening times can be obtained from the *Association Nationale des Exploitants des Cavernes Aménagées pour le Tourisme* (A.N.E.C.A.T.), 12 rue Lamande, 75017 Paris. Caves are also marked on Michelin and IGT maps and are described in detail in the relevant Michelin green guides.

River gorges, like grottoes, are found in limestone areas, and the largest and most impressive are therefore found in the southern part of the country, cutting through the *causses* on the southern edge of the Massif Central and the Alpes Maritimes.

The largest and most spectacular gorge in France, and for that matter, in the whole of Europe, is the Grand Canyon du Verdon on the limestone plateau of Haute-Provence. It is over 20 kilometres long and in places reaches a depth of 800 metres. In the same general region there are several other gorges, though on nothing like the same scale as that of the Verdon: the Gorges de Daluis, Gorges du Cians, Gorges du Loup and Gorges de la Vesubie. The Gorges de Daluis are notable for the heather colour of their rock-faces. Near Mont Ventoux, not far from Orange, are the Gorges de la Nesque, which cut a picturesque path through the limestone plateau of the Vaucluse.

After Verdon the finest river gorges in France are those of the Tarn, and including the adjacent Gorges de la Jonte and Gorges de la Dourbie. 50 kilometres long, the Gorges du Tarn have an endless variety of exciting scenery, and it is possible to go through a part of the gorges in a small, flat-bottomed boat. There are six other notable gorges in the same area.

In the Ardèche, the Gorges de l'Ardèche are a great tourist attraction. Other gorges on the Massif Central are those of the Allier (through which the train from Paris to Nîmes passes), the

Gorges de la Truyère and the Gorges de la Sioule. There are others, but they are mostly of more modest proportions.

The many gorges and deep river valleys have made possible the building of a great number of dams in the more mountainous regions of the Massif Central. These are mainly used for generating electricity, but they have another important function in that they control flood water on fast flowing rivers. Even the River Loire used to have its gorge: situated just above Roanne it is in the course of being flooded after a great dam has been built across the river at its lower end.

Beaches

The coast line of France offers a great variety of beaches. Some parts, like the Côte d'Azur and the small stretch from Biarritz to St. Jean de Luz, are to be numbered among the play-grounds of Europe and are so popular that they become hopelessly overcrowded in the height of the season. By comparison, the vast sandy expanses of the Aquitaine coast still offer some elbow room, as do the beaches of Brittany, Normandy and Picardy. The latter two offer inviting stretches of fine sand and shingle with bright, bracing resorts like Le Touquet, Deauville and Trouville. Only the climate prevents them from becoming more popular. A particularly attractive stretch is that between Dieppe and Le Havre, where high chalk cliffs tower above the shingle beaches.

Brittany, a region with strong maritime connections, has its own special attractions with many sandy coves cutting into the rocky coast. Despite the great popularity of the area, one can still find solitude even at the height of the holiday season. On the south side of Brittany, facing the Bay of Biscay, the areas of sand only increase as one approaches the mouth of the Loire. Quiberon Bay and its peninsula have long golden beaches, but the jewel on the crown is la Baule on the Côte d'Amour, a crescent of fine, yellow sand some 8 kilometres long.

South of the Loire, in a climate said to rival that of the Côte d'Azure, is the 'Cote de Lumière' of the Vendée, a series of long sandy shores backed by pines and dunes. Les Sables d'Olonne is the premier resort on this coast, with a huge, gentle beach. There are further stretches of sand as far as the Charente-Maritime coast, which is some 410 kilometres in length. The rocky shores of the 'Côte Sauvage' with its islands of Ré and Oléron are followed by another expanse of sandy beaches which start 13 kilometres to the north of Royan and extend into the mouth of the Gironde. Royan itself, with a huge sheltered beach, is the most modern seaside resort in France, and justly popular.

The Beaches of France

From the Gironde to the Adour, over a total of 270 kilometres, stretch the enormous beaches of the Landes. This area of coastal dunes and lagoons was forested in the 19th Century, producing what was then the largest man-made forest in Europe. On the seaward side of the dunes, which are in places several hundred feet high, long beaches of white sand reach into the distance as far as the eye can see. Atlantic rollers make these beaches difficult for swimming, but they are ideal for surfing. Access to the beaches is by way of a string of resorts and camp sites which shelter amid the pines behind the dunes; the most popular ones are Lacanau-Ocean, Biscarrosse-Plage, Mimizan-Plage, Hossegor. Roughly at the mid-point of the Landes coast is the Bassin d'Arcachon, famous for its oysters. Arcachon itself is a fine holiday resort.

From the Adour to the Spanish border lies a short, very fashionable, stretch of coast, well-known for its resorts at Biarritz and St. Jean-de-Luz. Made famous by King Edward VII and other notables of Europe in the 19th Century, it still enjoys enormous popularity.

The Mediterranean is virtually tideless, and because of this, and the superb climate, it enjoys a greater popularity with sun-seekers than does most of the Atlantic coast. In the last 20 years the coast of Languedoc-Roussillon has undergone a massive transformation. The already popular beaches and their attendant resorts have been systematically developed into great holiday centres like Valras-Plage, Narbonne-Plage, Port-Leucate, Port-Bacares, St. Cyprien-Plage. These are ambitious, 20th-century resorts with large, boldly-designed hotel and apartment complexes where every type of watersport is catered for.

The stretch of coast belonging to Provence is mainly taken up by the estuary of the Rhône, the Camargue, and there is thus only limited access to the sea.

East of Marseilles is France's most popular stretch of coast, the Riviera or Côte d'Azur. Its fame is based both on its incomparable climate, and on the many beauty spots both inland and on the coast. It is indeed outstandingly beautiful, with rocky cliffs, little bays and the occasional beaches, interspersed with lively resorts that have much to offer. There is something here for everyone, but it does get very crowded in the season, especially in the most fashionable part, from St. Tropez to Menton. It is said that in July and August four times as many people descend on the area as can comfortably be accommodated, and it is thus imperative that you book in advance.

Mountains

The major mountain range are the Alps, extending from Lac Léman (Lake Geneva) in the north almost to the Riviera in the south, and from the Swiss/Italian border in the east to the Rhône in the west. The northern sector contains Europe's highest mountain, Mont Blanc, with a height of 4,807 metres and the Barre des Écrins, which rises to 4,103 metres. Further south, the Maritime Alps are not so high but are still impressive, being particularly attractive for their Mediterranean character. In the summer, the motorist can drive the length of the French Alps, crossing pass after pass, each opening up breathtaking views. In the winter, the Savoie and Dauphiné Alps in particular are completely given over to winter sports. Everyone has heard of Courchevel, Val Thorens or Alpe d'Huez, but there are scores of other resorts all well equipped with ski lifts, ski schools and very modern hotels and holiday apartments. In the summer leisure activities centre around sailing and swimming in the lakes of Savoie, mountain walking with or without guides and serious mountain climbing. There are two spectacular national Nature Parks, La Vanoise and Les Écrins, both of which have strict policies of protection towards animals and plants. There are also two Regional Nature Parks, Le Vercors and Le Queyras, which have been set up for the promotion of outdoor activities, regional economy, culture and environment.

Separating France from Spain are the Pyrénées, not as high as the Alps but nevertheless reaching around 3,400 metres at their highest. They rise abruptly from the lowlands of Gascony and Languedoc and do not have an extensive area of gradually ascending foot-hills in the way the Alps have. The Pyrénées are a favourite haunt of nature lovers for their wild beauty and their peculiar fauna. Bears, civet and ibex can be seen, and myriads of butterflies. The Pyrénées Occidentales National Park, which encompasses about 72 kilometres near the Spanish border, is open to all visitors. Mountaineering, salmon fishing and skiing in winter are well established outdoor activities.

The mountains of the Franche-Comté, the Jura, which extend

The Mountains and Rivers of France

the length of the French/Swiss border, are modest in height (a little over 1,700 metres at their highest), but their steep wooded slopes and fast-flowing streams give them a character all of their own. Cycling, riding and walking are favourite outdoor activities.

The mountains of the *Vosges*, the French counterpart of the Black Forest and very similar in character with their densely wooded slopes and many lakes, also reach a modest height only. They are a popular holiday venue for walkers, dinghy sailors and campers and offer the additional attraction of the Alsace wine growing regions along their east-facing slopes.

Finally, but certainly not least in importance among France's mountain regions, there are the peaks of the Massif Central. An ancient volcanic block with the remains of many extinct volcanoes, the Massif rises to its highest point near Clermont

Ferrand in Auvergne (Puy de Sancy, 1,886 metres). The Massif Central is not an Alpine landscape of soaring peaks and eternal snow but one of accessible high hills, plateaux and gorges, sometimes bare and rocky but mostly green with pastures, fir and beech trees, chestnuts and poplars. It is a marvellous holiday area for walking, riding, canoeing and fishing. The Auvergne-Volcanoes Regional Nature Park is in two parts: the northern part in the Monts Dômes west of Clermont Ferrand, the southern part in Cantal.

National Parks, Regional Nature Parks and Nature Reserves

National Parks

The six National Parks of France are not parks in the accepted sense but very large, comparatively remote regions where flora and fauna are protected. They are open to all lovers of nature — walkers, naturalists, photographers, skiers — but they do not provide 'amusements'. A network of well-marked paths can be used on foot, on horseback or on skies, depending on the season. Guided walks and climbs, ski courses, photo safaris and other outdoor activities are organised, and huts provide basic accommodation for long-distance ramblers and mountaineers. Guide books and advice can be collected from information centres. Each National Park has a 'peripheral zone', which takes in villages and hamlets where hotels, inns and campsites can be found and where more general pastimes like boating, canoeing, swimming or pony trekking can be pursued. The six National Parks shown on the map following are:—

Parc national des Cévennes, in the *départements* of Lozère and Gard, with Florac roughly at the centre, features rich and diverse flora, some threatened species of birds, like the golden eagle, eagle owl, peregrine falcon and vultures together with wild boar and roe-deer. Information can be obtained from Parc National des Cévennes, Chateau de Florac, B.P.4, 48400 Florac. Information centres in the summer are at Pont de Montvert, Meyreuis, Saint Jean du Gard, Le Vigan, Genolhac and Villefort.

Parc National des Écrins in the *départements* of Isère and Hautes Alpes, north-east of Gap, has typically alpine flora and fauna, and the park is exceptionally rich in insects. Information can be obtained from Parc National des Écrins, 7, rue du Colonel Roux, B.P.142, 05004 Gap Cedex and documentation and help with accommodation from Maison du Parc, 05290 Vallouise. Information centres are found at Bourg d'Oisans, Entraigues, La Grave, Monétier, Briançon, Chateauroux, Champoléon and La Chapelle en Valgaudemar.

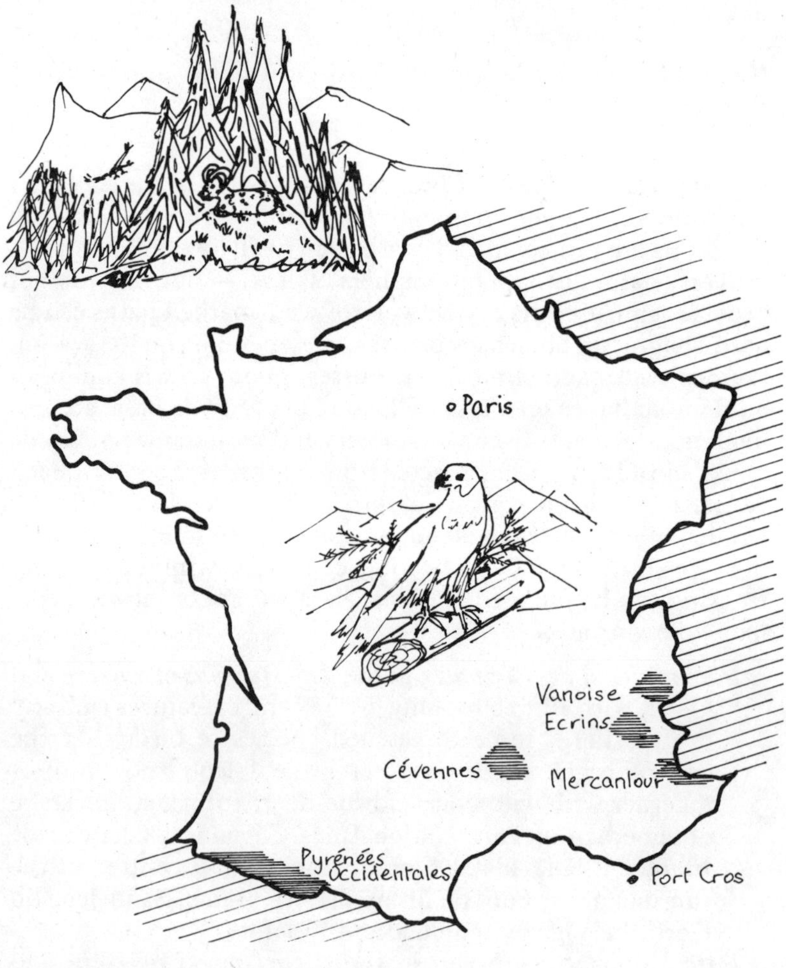

The National Parks of France

Parc National du Mercantour lies in the *départements* of Alpes Maritimes and Alpes de Haute Provence, roughtly south-east of Barcelonette, along the Italian border and features both Mediterranean and alpine flora. The fauna includes chamoix, moufflons, ibex, marmot, ermine, owls and golden eagles. Information may be had from Parc National du Mercantour, 13, rue Maccarani, 06000 Nice. Information centres are at Bévera, Vésubie, Tinée, Haut Var, Haut Verdon and Ubaye.

Parc National de Port Cros is on the island of Port Cros in the Hautes Alpes, north-east of Gap, has typically alpine flora and fauna, and the park is exceptionally rich in hoopoes and bee-eaters, and so is the neighbouring island of Porquerolles. Information may be obtained from Parc National de Port Cros, 50, avenue Gambetta, 83400 Hyères.

Parc National des Pyrénées Occidentales lies south of Pau, about 100 kilometres along the Spanish border at a height of from 1,100 to 3,298 metres. Remarkable wildlife includes brown bear, wild goat, muskrat, griffon vulture, lammergeyer, ptarmigan, marmot, ermine, wild boar, fox, marten and otter. Rare flowers abound. Information may be obtained from Parc National des Pyrénées Occidentales, Route de Pau, B.P.300, 65013 Tarbes and local *Syndicats d'Initiative.*

Parc National de la Vanoise is in the *département* of Savoie, south-east of Chambéry. Again it is a high-altitude park (1,250 to 3,835 metres) with 107 peaks exceeding 3000 metres. Together with the Italian National Park, which it adjoins, this is the largest nature reserve in Western Europe. It has a very rich alpine flora, while the abundant fauna includes ibex, badger, fox, marmot, ermine, ptarmigan, birds of prey and many song birds. Information is available from Parc National de la Vanoise, 135, rue du Docteur Julliand, B.P.000, 73003 Chambéry and local *Syndicats d'Initiative.*

Regional Nature Parcs

There are some 21 of these on the mainland of France, as shown on the following map, and 4 more in the process of being set up. In contrast to the National Parks, which are generally in remote, sparsely populated areas and have been created with the primary

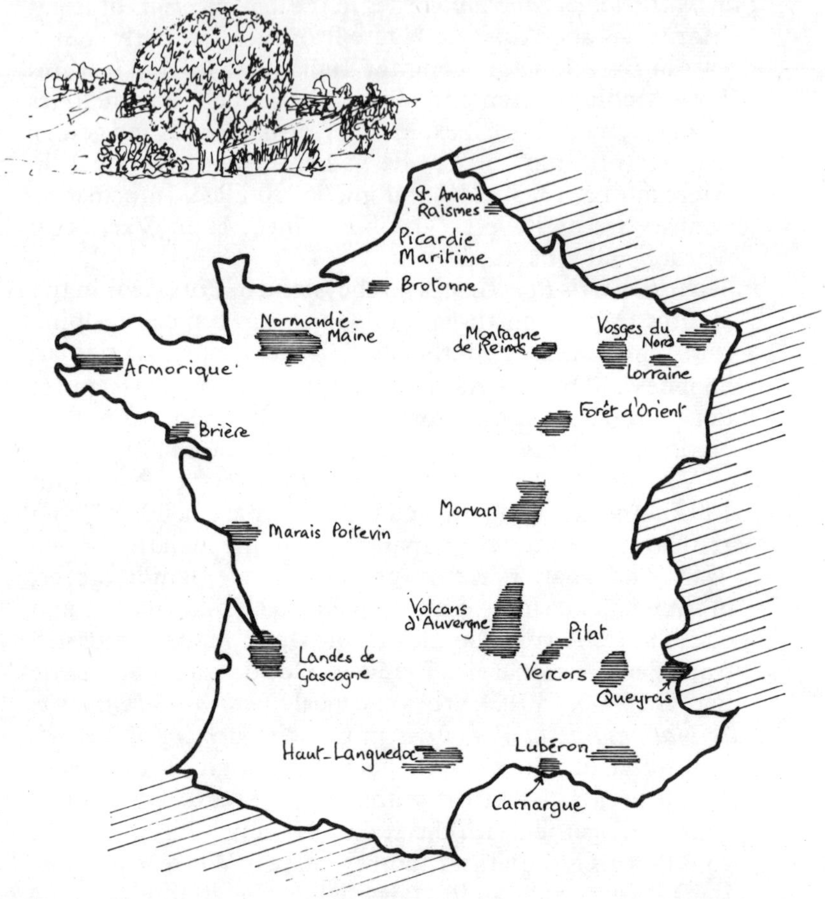

Regional Nature Parks in France

aim of nature and wildlife protection, the Regional Nature Parks extend over more populated regions and are intended to attract visitors and thereby help revitalize the social and commercial life as well as preserve the ecology and cultural heritage of a region. Some of their features are meeting and conference centres for talks and seminaries, open-air and indoor museums, animal parks, marked footpaths and organised sports activities. Each park offers an annual, comprehensive programme. Full information can be obtained from Fédération des Parcs Naturels de France, 4, rue de Stockholm, 75008 Paris.

The *Nature Reserves* of France are too numerous to be listed here. There are some 55 on the mainland of France, all of them are relatively small and specialized and some are open to the public in a limited way only. This may mean either at certain times only, or with a guide or special permit. They have been set up for the preservation of rare or threatened species of plants or animals, or even of geological formations. Details can be obtained from the French Government Tourist Office, address on p.185.

16. SPORTS

Cycling

Cycling is an excellent way to get about in the French countryside, providing you avoid the worst of the mountain roads, since traffic density off the main roads is light. The usual rules apply: riding in single file, have adequate lighting at night and use cycle tracks where they are provided. An adequate insurance, covering both accident and third party risk, is an esential when cycling. The ordinary holiday insurance does not necessarily cover cycling accidents, so you should check this very carefully.

Bicycles (*vélos*) can be hired at some French railway stations and from cycle shops in most towns. Some of the Cross-Channel ferries will transport bicycles free of charge, and they may be transported cheaply by French Railways and on some bus routes. For further information on cycling in Europe you can write to the Touring Department, Cyclists Touring Club, Cotterell House, 69 Meadow, Godalming, Surrrey, GU7 3HS.

Walking

France is not, like Germany or Austria, a country with a profusion of well-marked and well-kept footpaths and a population that takes to boots and rucksacks every weekend to tramp along them. In Austria you can spend a whole holiday clambering up and down mountains and marching through forests and get medals for it: bronze, silver or gold, depending on how many kilometers you have clocked up. Not so in France. The French are not, as a nation, enthusiastic hikers, and there is no tradition of Sunday hiking with the family. No coachloads and carloads of purposeful, energetic nature lovers equipped with sticks and rainwear spew themselves out on parking lots in the middle of forests and at the foot of mountain slopes. When the French get out of their cars they look forward to a picnic, not a strenuous walk!

This does not mean that *nobody* walks at all, or that no provisions whatsoever are made. Walking is not a *pre*-occupation, but simply an occupation in which quite a few people are interested. There are several thousand miles of marked tracks across the countryside, but they are long-distance routes planned for walking tours from one part of the country to the other. To use them, the walker certainly needs to be more confident than on the well-frequented, short-distance circuits in Austria's holiday resorts. They are not meticulously marked at frequent intervals and the walker will not be likely to meet many other walkers. Nor will he encounter many knowledgeable locals to whom he can turn for advice.

The routes referred to are the *Sentiers de Grande Randonnée* (long-distance foot paths), administered by the Comité National des Sentiers de Grande Randonné, 92 rue de Clignancourt 75883 Paris. This organisation publishes some 130 *'Topoguides'* (in French), illustrated with extracts from the IGN 1:25,000 scale maps, which cover a total of about 20,000 kilometres of straight and circular itineraries. These can take anything from one week to three weeks to cover. Details are given on places of interest along the way and on where to find shelters, hotels, shops, water, camp sites, etc. All the *Grande Randonnée* footpaths are shown on the IGN Map 903 *Sentiers de Grande Randonnée*. This map, as well as the *Topoguides*, can be ordered from McCarta Ltd., 122 Kings Cross Road, London WC1X 9DS.

Footpaths in high-mountain areas, i.e. in Savoie, Haute-Savoie, Isère, Hautes-Alpes and Pyrénées involve stretches of advanced grades of difficulty. It cannot be emphasised enough that inexperienced walkers with inadequate equipment should not embark on such walks, which should strictly be classified as climbs. Anyone contemplating this skilled type of mountain walking would do well to approach the Club Alpin Francais, 7, rue de la Boétie, 75008 Paris, with a view to membership. The club publishes information of value to climbers, and members have priority in using the club's mountain huts (marked on Michelin maps as *Refuge C.A.F.*) The C.A.F. also runs climbing schools.

Information on local walks and, in mountain regions, the

availability of mountain guides can be obtained from the local *Syndicat d'Initiative* on the spot.

Horse Riding and Pony-Trekking

In recent years, there has been ample evidence of the fact that the French have taken to horse riding as a major sport. It has not been as easy as in countries like Great Britain, since there are large parts of France in which the horse is still regarded simply as a working animal. However, the exciting possibilities of making journeys by horse across the wide open spaces of the French countryside could hardly be ignored for long.

It is now very common to see groups of riders making their way through the forests and along the less frequented paths on their way from one staging post to the next. Accommodation (in many cases rather basic) provided at regular intervals makes this kind of holiday really attractive to the young.

It is possible, too, to take courses in learning to ride before engaging in more adventurous activities and the French Youth Hostels Association is a leading organisation in this field. Their address in *Fédération Unie des Auberges de Jeunesses*, 11 bis Rue de Milan, Paris 9 and they will send all details of their plans for the year.

Local riding schools are all known to the local *Syndicats d'Initiative* and there is also an organisation entitled *Association nationale pour le tourisme equestre*, 12, rue de Parc-Royal, 75003 Paris, which can give all the most important details about overnight accommodation, maps, rallies, preparation and making of treks. (Please enclose an international Reply Coupon if you write for details). Some of the recently introduced *Loisirs Accueil* booking offices (see p.10 and addresses p.187) can arrange riding and pony-trekking holidays, which will be featured in their brochures.

Fishing

Fishing is a national obsession in France. Every canal, pond, lake, river and stream is a potential hunting ground for anglers, and, if it happens to be private, has to be protected by notices saying *Pêche privée* or *Pêche interdite*. If there is no sign of a notice anywhere you can assume that it is alright to go ahead, but you should, nevertheless, have a licence (*permis de pêche*). This only costs a few francs and can be bought at a sports shop or a bait-and-tackle shop. If in doubt, ask the *Syndicat d'Initiative* or, in a village, the local café proprietor. Despite some inevitable pollution, the waters of France are full of fish. Common freshwater species are pike, perch, carp, roach, char, gudgeon and grayling. Trout can be caught in the mountain streams and salmon in rivers like the Allier and Loire. There are restrictions on fishing for certain species and on permitted minimum size, which may differ from one *département* to another. There is also a closed season. One should enquire about these matter at the time of buying the licence.

Golf

Golf has become a major sport in France in recent years, and there are good courses at La Baule, Le Touquet, St. Cyprien, St-Jean-de-Luz, Biarritz, Hossegor, Cannes, Evian and Clermont-Ferrand, and others are being built all the time. More details can be obtained from the French Golf Federation, 11, rue de Bassano, 75003 Paris.

Canoeing

The tremendous number of streams, rivers and canals in France make the country a paradise for the canoeist. Tests of skill range from the fast-flowing mountain streams in the Alps, the Pyrénées, the Vosges, the Jura and the Massif Central to the gentler streams of the lowlands and the still waters of the canals, which are ideal highways for the long-distance paddler. All French rivers are graded, according to difficulty, from I to IV. Great care must be exercised on Grade IV rivers, and no inexperienced canoeist should venture on them without expert advice and help.

The *Fédération Française de Canoe-Kayak*, 87, quai de la Marne, 94340 Joinville, can be approached for details on canoeing in France (enclose International Reply coupon), or for information on a particular location the regional Tourist Committee (see addresses on p.000) Some of the *Loisirs Accueil* booking offices (see p.000 and addresses p.000) have canoeing courses among their activity holidays.

Sailing and Windsurfing

Sailing is a major sport in France and is indulged in wherever there is suitable water. The large number of artificial and natural inland lakes ensure that there is scarcely a part of the country where a small sailing yacht cannot be put afloat. There are a considerable number of camping sites located on such stretches of water which lend themselves ideally to launching a boat. A good camping guide should indicate this possibility. Apart from the lakes formed by large dams, some of the rivers have stretches of water ideal for watersports, especially near larger towns. They are usually brought about by the building of a weir or low barrage which holds the water back, but still allows a current to flow. There is an excellent *Centre Nautique* like this on the Allier at Vichy and another on the Loire at Blois and there are many others including some on the Seine. On many of these lakes or *Centres Nautiques* there is invariably a section set aside for water ski-ing. Since there is usually a yacht club in such places (*Club de Voile*) the visitor can apply to the secretary before going ahead to launch his boat.

Large parts of the coastal waters of France are ideal for small boat sailing. To start with, the Mediterranean coast in the Languedoc-Rousillon area is first class. You can launch from the beach, but you can also use one of the many harbours. The seas can get very rough, especially if the mistral blows, but there are no tides and currents to cause difficulties. Further along, on the Riviera coast, the opportunities to launch a small boat are more restricted and the waters get very crowded. So do the dinghy parks or small stretches of beach. In this area the windsurfer is likely to have a better chance of success.

The Biscay Coast, being tidal and more exposed to strong winds calls for a more resolute type of sailor. The Landes coast has large waves on calm days and is more suitable for surf riding than sailing. But there are a number of sheltered lagoons behind the dunes. St Jean de Luz and Henday by the Spanish border are more suitable, because they have sheltered harbours. Otherwise Hossegor and Arcachon, which provide sheltered inland water at high tide, are the favourite spots.

On the Gironde estuary Royan is outstanding, with a large flat sheltered beach for launching, then comes La Rochelle (premier yachting centre on the French Atlantic coast) and La Baule, a very popular dinghy sailors resort with wide, flat sands as well as a protected harbour. Quiberon and many of the other resorts of the south Britanny coast are ideal for dinghies, but the major centre on this coast is the famous sailing school at the Ile de Glénans. There is good sailing in most of the small inlets and river estuaries of the Brittany coast. The River Rance with its tidal barrage has now a sizeable inland lake near Dinard at high water, but the open water to the north which encompasses the Channel Islands and the west coast of the Cotentin Peninsula has enormous tides and is not ideal for dinghy sailing, certainly not for the inexperienced.

The Normandy coast, between the Cotentin Peninsula and Le Havre, though somewhat exposed in bad weather, is quite suitable for small-boat sailing, and there are a number of major yacht harbours, like Grandcamp, Port-en-Bessin, Courseuilles, Deauville and Honfleur. Le Havre, too, has a large yacht harbour, but the Seine estuary is not the most favoured water for small boats. Nor is the Normandy coast further north, which has high cliffs and big tides. Occasionally there are suitable beaches for launching dinghies in fine weather, but on the whole this is not the place to take small boats. Wind surfers on the other hand, take a totally different view of the matter.

Due to their lightness and ease of handling in and out of the water, the wind surfer has become the ideal item of watersports equipment for taking on a car-top and putting afloat in minutes in any suitable piece of water. The wind surfer is not expensive and does not appear to give its operator undue difficulties after the first anxious lessons. It is clearly the holiday sailing boat of the future, and France offers infinite opportunities, inland and on the coasts, for putting it into action.

The French Government Tourist Office in London publishes a factsheet on Yachting and Boating with some details on temporary import of boats, regulations, canal navigation and addresses to which to turn for more information, charts and guides. A list of companies offering sailing/cruising holidays in France, as well as a list of French boat hire companies is also available (please send 50p in stamps!) Some of the *Loisirs Accueil* booking offices (see p.10 and addresses p.187) feature sailing, cruising and windsurfing courses among their activity holidays.

Inland waterways

With 7,500 kilometres of rivers and canals France has one of the most extensive and attractive waterway networks in Europe. Commercial traffic is heavy over certain stretches and should be treated with caution and respect, but the delightful Canal de Nantes à Brest in Brittany is used exclusively for pleasure navigation and its locks have to be operated by the yachtsmen themselves. There are no special skills needed for canal cruising except alertness in traffic, patience in locks and a knowledge of the basic regulations. Canals pass through delightful towns which offer opportunities for shopping, sightseeing and eating out. The Canal du Midi, which is the link between the Atlantic and the Mediterranean, passes through the best climatic region of France.

The majority of readers would probably be more interested in hiring a boat on a canal or river than in taking their own, and for them there are a number of companies in the UK who offer canal-cruise holidays in France, Blakes Holidays and Hoseasons Holidays being just two. A full list with addresses is available from the French Government Tourist Office. Their factsheet mentioned in 'Sailing and Windsurfing' above also applies to cruising on inland waterways and contains information, and sources of information, for anyone who wants to take his own boat. Some of the *Loisirs Accueil* booking offices (see p.10 and addresses p.187) offer boat hire on rivers and canals among their activity holidays.

17. MISCELLANY

Rail Travel in France

The French rail system is extensive and efficient, serving 6,000 destinations. It runs the world's fastest train (known as TGV = *train à grande vitesse*) between Paris and Lyon. French Railways offer a car hire and bicycle hire service to rail users, and a *France Vacance* rail rover ticket for unlimited travel for 7 days, 15 days or 1 months. Full details may be had from French Railways, 179 Piccadilly, London W1V 0BA. A word of warning about rail tickets bought in France at French railway stations: find out in advance whether the train on which you intend to travel is just an ordinary train or a 'special' train, i.e. high-speed, express or first-class-only. As in most other European countries, a supplement is payable on such trains, and the man at the ticket counter has to allow for this when issuing your ticket. If you board one of these trains without a supplement ticket and an inspector comes your way, he will not necessarily fine you, but he will certainly make you pay the supplement on the spot. You will definitely be fined, however, if you have failed to date-stamp your rail ticket in one of the orange machines installed at platform entrances, which have replaced the 'man at the barrier'. Date Stamping, or *compostage*, is a relatively recent system introduced at all railway stations. Tickets are not dated and can be bought and used at any time but must be date-stamped *before* the user boards the train. Fines for not doing so amount to 20% of the fare, with a minimum of 24F!

Travel by Coach

There are not many long-distance coaches operating in France, with the exception of Europabus (information from British Rail Travel Centres), but there are, generally, very good local services between towns, which are not particularly expensive. Taking a local bus is a certain way for the driver to relax for a change, and you can forget parking problems in strange towns. Moreover, you will get a little taste of the local atmosphere as the local population joins and leaves the bus. Ask at the local *Syndicat d'Initiative* for a timetable and fare details.

Car Hire

You can hire a car in advance, to be waiting for you on arrival in France, directly through one of the many international car hire firms like Hertz, Avis, or Godfrey Davis, or through a travel agent, or motoring organisation. If you fly or go by train, most airlines as well as French Railways offer a car hire service. Alternatively, a car can be hired on the spot through one of the companies mentioned, which have booking offices throughout France. A list of addresses can be obtained from their headquarters, see p.189. French offices of Avis are marked and listed on the map *La France du Voyage* obtainable from Sofitel (see p.35). Not infrequently you get a better deal by pre-booking a hire car in the UK. The weekly hire-charge, through one of the well-known companies, for the lowest-category car (e.g. Renault 5) is about 1200F, including unlimited mileage, but excluding petrol. The lower age limit for car hire in France is normally 21.

Toilet Facilities

What is a perennial problem to foreign visitors is solved by a large proportion of the French male population with the help of trees, hedges, church walls, town walls, any walls and a total disregard for onlookers! In fact, some provision has been made for men for many years by the erection of the well-known little concrete or iron edifices placed in strategic spots.

Public conveniences of a rather more sophisticated type for the population at large are still not very numerous in France. In towns they can often be found in squares where markets are held or from where buses leave, near churches and in public parks. Success may also be encountered at railway stations, in big department stores, hypermarkets, some Métro stations in Paris, airports, and some public buildings such as museums and casinos, but not generally at petrol stations. Cafés and restaurants, of course, are always equipped with this desirable facility, but you cannot just walk in and out of a café without at least having a drink. If you take your family of four for refreshment and relief it can become a rather expensive exercise (and it defeats the object!) Charges in public loos are generally 50 centimes these days. If there is no fixed charge, give the attendant a tip of 50 centimes anyway. The hole-in-the-ground affair called *installation à la turque*, which is so dreaded by foreign visitors, is, fortunately, on the way out. If you should happen to come across one, regard it as an enlightening encounter with a fast disappearing species.

Some thoughtful *Syndicats d'Initiative* have taken the trouble to mark toilets on the free towns plans, e.g. Boulogne, but experience shows that the visitor should not rely on the facility being available for use either at all hours of the day and night or at all times of the year.

Son et Lumière

It has become universally popular to illuminate important and historical buildings at night in order to extend their visual attractions past the daylight hours. In France it has long been common to do so during the summer tourist season, and there can be few among the many important châteaux and walled towns which are not given this treatment. It is one of the outstanding features of the Loire valley, and even whole cities like Avignon and Carcassonne are turned into veritable film sets of molten gold against black velvet.

So much for the '*lumière*' part of it. The '*son*', or sound, is something which is very French in its conception. It consists of music, poetry readings and even performances with actors in historical costume recalling the former glory of the site. It is certainly worth going to one or two of these performances, which can be a delightful way of spending a warm summer evening. Many of the perfomances are in English as well as French, often on the same evening but at a different time, or on alternate days. The local *Syndicat d'Initiative* will provide details.

Fairs

The summer scene in rural France is enlivened by the appearance, in village after village, of the travelling amusement park or fairground. Posters will appear overnight on walls and trees, while leaflets stuck under your windscreen wipers will announce the '*Grande Foire*' or '*Grande Fête*' or '*Parc d'Attractions*', and sure enough a few days later a convoy of vehicles will arrive and purposeful young men with dirty hands and spanners will commence setting up shooting booths and coconut shies, hot-dog stalls, dodgem cars, roundabouts and roller-coasters, and sometimes even a dance hall. It is all done on quite a small scale, and even modest villages have a square or suitable space in the middle large enough to accommodate a few amusements. For two or three days, while the fair operates in the late afternoon and evening (not during the day, note!) the young people of the village and its adjoining hamlets, plus a sprinkling of holiday makers, converge on the square to enjoy loud music, *frites*, beer, and the occasional exhilerating ride in something that goes bump or swish, while the smaller children spend their pocket money on ice cream, candy floss and cheap trinkets.

Sometimes such a fair is connected with local celebrations like a Saint's Day and features rather more ambitious spectacles such as shooting competitions or fireworks. It is all an essential element of the French countryside in summer, and if you see a poster up somewhere advertising a local fair you should not miss the chance to drop in on it.

Annual Events

A list of annual events in France can be obtained from the F.G.T.O. in London (address p.185). This is published in March and covers the current year. Some of the most important events are:

Monte Carlo Rally — January
Nice Carnival — February
Cannes Film Festival — May
Monaco Grand Prix — May
Le Mans 24 hours — June
Tour de France — July
Paris Motor Show — September/October

Note: actual dates vary each year.

Public Holidays

French public holidays, on which banks and (most) shops are closed are:

New Year's Day (January 1)
Easter (Sunday and Monday)
Labour Day (May 1)
VE Day (May 8)
Ascension Day (May, 39 days after Easter)
Whitsun (May or June, Sunday and Monday)
Bastille Day (July 14)
Assumption Day (August 15)
All Saints Day (November 1)
Remembrance Day (November 11)
Christmas Day (December 25)

School Holidays

French school holidays fall into the same pattern as they do in the UK: Easter, summer and Christmas, with short half-term holidays in between. The dates are staggered throughout the regions. The long summer holidays, during which the whole of France seems to be on the move, are the most important for the visitor, because they affect traffic density and the availability of accommodation. Depending on the region, they fall somewhere between the last week in June and the second week in September.

Comparative Clothes and Shoe Sizes

Shoes

Children		*Adults*		
GB	France	GB	US	France
3	19	1	2½	33
4	20	2	3½	34/35
5	21/22	3	4½	36
6	23	4	5½	37
7	24	5	6½	38
8	25/26	6	7½	39/40
9	27	7	8½	41
10	28	8	9½	42

11	29	9	10½	43
12	30/31	10	11½	44
13	32	11	12½	45
		12	13½	46

Men's Shirts (collar)

GB/US	France
14	35/36cm
14½	37cm
15	38cm
15½	39/40cm
16	41cm
16½	42cm
17	43cm
17½	44cm

Men's suits/coats

GB/US	France
36	46
38	48
40	50
42	52
44	54
46	56

Ladies' dresses, skirts, coats etc.

GB	US	France
10	8	36
12	10	38
14	12	40
16	14	42
18	16	44
20	18	46
22	20	48
24	22	50

18. USEFUL ADDRESSES

French Government Tourist Office
178 Piccadilly
London W1V OAL
Tel. 01-491 7622
(if writing for printed information, lists, brochures etc. enclose 50p in stamps)

French Railways
179 Piccadilly
London W1V OBA
Tel. 01-493 4451

French Consulate General
24 Rutland Gate,
Londn SW7 IPH
Tel. 01-581 5292

Automobile Association
Overseas Touring Section
Fanum House,
Basingstoke, Hants
RG21 2EA
Tel. Basingstoke (0256) 20123

Gîtes de France
178 Piccadilly
London W1V OPQ
(Write for detail of membership (enclosing s.a.e.)

Fédération Nationale des Gîtes de France
35 rue Godot-de-Mauroy
75009 Paris

Comités Regionaux de Tourisme

These Regional Tourist Offices can be contacted in writing (no personal callers) for information on regions:

Ile de France: Comité Régional de Tourisme, 101 rue de Vaugirard, F-75006 — Paris, France.

Alsace-Vosges-Lorraine: Comité Régional de Tourisme, 5 place de la République, F-67073 — Strasbourg, France.

Aquitaine: Comité Régional de Tourisme, 24 Allées de Tourny, F-33000 — Bordeaux, France.

Auvergne: Comité de Tourisme, B.P. 395, F-63000 — Clermont-Ferrand, France.

Brittany: Comité Régional de Tourisme, B.P. 2275, F-35000 — Rennes, France.

Burgundy: Comité Régional de Tourisme, Préfecture, F-21034 — Dijon Cédex, France.

Champagne-Ardenne: Comité Régional de Tourisme, 2bis Boulevard Vaubécourt, F-51000 — Châlons-sur-Marne, France.

Corsica: Comité Régional de Tourisme, B.P.162, F-20178 — Ajaccio, France.

French Alps-Savoy: Comité de Tourisme, 11ter, avenue de Lyon, F-73000 — Chambéry, France.

French Alps-Dauphiny: Comité Régional de Tourisme, BP 227, F-38019 — Grenoble, France.

Franche-Comté: Comité Régional de Tourisme, Place de la 1ère Armée Française, F-25041 — Besançon, France.

Languedoc-Roussillon: Comité Régional de Tourisme, 12 rue Foch, F-34000 — Montpellier, France.

Limousin: Comité Régional de Tourisme, 8 Cours Bugeaud, F-8700 — Limoges, France.

Loire Valley/Touraine: Comité Dépt. de Tourisme, Préfecture d'Indre-et-Loire, F-37032 — Tours Cédex.

Midi-Pyrénées: Comité Régional de Tourisme, 3 rue de L'Esquile, F-31000 — Toulouse, France.

Nord Pas-de-Calais: Comité Régional Tourisme, 157 Boulevard de la Liberté, F-59800 — Lille, France.

Normandy: Comité Régional de Tourisme, 35 rue Josephine, F-27022 — Evreux Cédex, France.

Picardy: Comité Régional de Tourisme, 9 rue Allart, BP 0342,

F-80003 — Amiens, France.
Poitou-Charentes: Comité Régional de Tourisme, B.P.56, F-86000 — Poitiers, France.
Provence: Comité Régional de Tourisme, 22a rue Louis-Maurel, F-13006 — Marseille, France.
Rhône Valley: Comité Régional de Tourisme, 5 Place de la Baleine, F-69005 — Lyon, France.
Riviera/Côte d'Azur: Comité Régional de Tourisme, 55 Promenade des Anglais, F-06000 — Nice, France.
Western Loire: Comité Régional de Tourisme, 3 Place St-Pierre, F-44000 — Nantes Cédex, France.

The Paris Central Tourist Office is for personal callers and is open every day, including Sundays and Public Holidays, from 9 a.m. till 10 p.m.:

Paris: Office de Tourisme, 127 avenue des Champs-Elysées, F-75008 — Paris France.

Loisirs-Accueil Booking Offices

These help with booking hotels, gîtes, activity holidays. Write for brochure.

Aquitaine (Dordogne): Loisirs-Accueil, 16 rue du Président Wilson, 24000 Périgueux, France. Tel. (53) 53 44 35, Telex 570335 CHACOPER.
Aquitaine (Gironde): Loisirs-Accueil, 21 cours de l'Intendance, 33000, Bordeaux, France. Tel (56) 52 61 40, Telex 54 1523 GIRTOUR.
Auvergne (Cantal): Loisirs-Accueil, BP 8, 15000 Aurillac, France. Tel. (71) 48 53 54.
Brittany (Ille et Vilaine): Loisirs-Accueil, 1 rue Martenot, 3500 Rennes, France. Tel (99) 02 97 41 or 02 97 42, Telex 730808 IVTOUR.
Champagne-Ardenne (Ardennes): Loisirs-Accueil, 18 avenue G-Corneau, 08000 Charleville, France. Tel (24) 56 00 63, Telex 8400 16 CHAMCO (specify 'Tourism').
Franche-Comté (Jura): Loisirs-Accueil, Préfecture, 39021 Lons-le-Saunier, France. Tel. (84) 24 19 6.
Franche-Comté (Haute-Saône): Loisirs-Accueil. B.P. 117, 70002 Vésoul Cédex, France, Tel (84) 754366, Telex 361250 F.

Languedoc-Roussillon (Aude:) Loisirs-Accueil, 70 rue Aimé Ramon, 11000 Carcassonne, France. Tel. (68) 47 09 06. Telex LARA 500370 F.
Languedoc-Roussillon (Lozèere): Loisirs-Accueil, BP no 4, 48002 Mende Cedex, France. Tel. (66) 65 34 55, Telex 480413.
Limousin (Corrèze): Loisirs-Accueil, Maison du Tourisme, Quai Baluze, 19000 Tulle, France. Tel. (55) 26 46 88, Telex CCITUL 590140
Limousin (Creuse/Haute-Vienne): Loisirs-Accueil, 16 place Jourdan, 87000 Limoges, France. Tel. (55) 34 70 11. Telex 580915 CECOMEX
Midi-Pyrénées (Haute-Garonne): Loisirs-Accueil, 4 rue Gabriel Péri, 31000 Toulouse, France. Tel. (61) 62 99 54.
Midi-Pyrénées (Gers): Loisirs-Accueil, Découverte de Gascogne, Maison des Agriculteurs, Route de Tarbes, 32003 Auch cédax, France. Tel. (62) 63 16 55 Extention ('poste') 310/306.
Midi-Pyrénées (Lot): Loisirs-Accueil, Chambre d'Agriculture, 430 Avenue Jean-Jaurès, 46000 Cahors, France. Tel. (65) 35 67 01. Telex CC1 Lot531427.
Midi-Pyrénées (Tarn): Loisirs-Accueil, Ancienne Préfecture, 81013 Albi, France. Tel. (63) 54 65 25. Telex 531412.
Midi-Pyrénées (Tarn-et-Garonne): Loisirs-Accueil, Hôtel des Intendants, Place du Maréchal Foch, 82000 Montauban, France. Tel. (63) 63 31 40. Telex 531705 F CCITGAR.
Picardy (Somme): Loisirs-Accueil, 21 rue Ernest Cauvin, 80000 Amiens, France. Tel. (22) 92 26 39. Telex 140754 CHAMCO AMIEN CDT
Poitou-Charentes (Charente): Loisirs-Accueil, Place Bouillaud, 16021 Angoulême, France. Tel. (45) 92 24 43. Telex 791607.
Poitour-Charentes (Charente-Maritime): Loisirs-Accueil 11bus rue des Augustins, 17000 La Rochelle, France. Tel. (46) 41 43 33, Telex 790712.
Provence (Hautes-Alpes): Loisirs-Accueil, 16 rue Carnot, 05000 Gap, France. Tel. (92) 51 39 49/52 14 23/51 31 45 (gîtes). Telex 400331.
Rhône Valley (Loire): Loisirs-Accueil, 5 Place Jean-Jaurès, 42021 Saint Etienne Cédex, France. Tel. (77) 33 15 39.
Savoy Alps (Savoie): Loisirs-Accueil, 5 rue du Château, 73000

Chambéry, France. Tel. (79) 85 01 09. Telex 320444 F.
Val De Loire/Centre (Loir-et-Cher): Loisirs-Accueil, 11 place du Château, 41000 Blois, France. Tel. (54) 78 55 50/78 4743. Telex 751375.
Val De Loire/Centre (Loiret): Loisirs-Accueil, 3 rue de la Bretonnerie, 45000 Orléans, France. Tel. (38) 62 04 88. Telex 780523.
Western Loire (Loire): Loisirs-Accueil, 34 rue de Strasbourg, 44000 Nantes, France. Tel. (40) 89 50 77. Telex 711505 CDTOUR.
Western Loire (Vendée): Loisirs-Accueil, Galerie Bonaparte, 8 place Napoleon, 85000 La Roche-sur-Yon, France. Tel. (51) 62 08 24. Telex 700747 F LOACVEN.

Car Hire Firms

Avis Rent-a-Car
Trident House
Station Road
Hayes, Middx.
Tel. 01-848 8765

Godfrey Davis Europcar
Bushey House
High Street
Bushey
Watford.
Tel. 01-828 7700

Hertz Rent-a-Car
40/44 The Broadway
London SW19
Tel. 01-542 6688

British Consulates and Embassies in France

PARIS 75008: 35 rue de Faubourg Saint-Honoré. Tel. (1) 266.91.42 (Embassy)
BIARRITZ 64200: Soc. Basque Automobile, Allées Paulmy. Tel. (59) 55.84.12
BORDEAUX 33081: 15 Cours de Verdun. Tel. (56) 52.28.35

BOULOGNE 62200: c/o British Rail, Gare Maritime, BP 327/1. Tel. (21) 30.25.11
CALAIS 62100: 11 rue Félix Cadras. Tel. (21) 34.45.48
CHERBOURG 50100: 8 rue Louis Philippe. Tel. (33) 53.14.46
DUNKIRK 59: c/o Jules Roy S.A., 6 Place de l'Yser. Tel. (20) 66.11.98
EPERNAY 51200: 37 avenue de Champagne. Tel. (26) 51.31.02
LE HAVRE 76600: 9 quai George V. Tel. (35) 42.27.47
LILLE 59800: 11 Square Dutilleul. Tel. (20) 52.87.90
LYONS 69288: 24 rue Childebert. Tel. (78) 37.59.67
MARSEILLES 13 (6e): 24 avenue du Prado. Tel. (91) 53.43.32
NANTES 44000: Westminster Bank, 6 rue Lafayette. Tel. (40) 71.08.50
STRASBOURG 67000: 10 rue du Général Castelneau. Tel. (88) 36.64.91
PERPIGNAN 66000: c/o Raquer France, 1 rue Buffon. Tel. (69) 34.94.04

Some useful addresses in the UK

French Consulate General (visa Dept.): College House, 29/31 Wright's Lane, London W8/01-937 1202 (open 9 a.m. to 1 p.m.).
French Consulate General: 24 Rutland Gate, London SW7 1PH/01-581 5292 (open from 9-15 a.m. to 1.15 p.m.).
French Consulate: 129 Queen Street, Cardiff CF1 6PS/0222-22 742.
French Consulate General: 7 Wemyss Place, Edinburgh EH3 6EL/O31-225 7954.
French Consulate: 39 Don Street, Saint Helier, Jersey CI/0534-26 256
French Consulate General: Cunard Building, Pier Head, Liverpool L3 1ET/051-236 8685.
French Embassy: 58 Knightsbridge, London SW1X 7JT/01-235 8080
French Embassy (Commercial Department): 12 Stanhope Gate, London W1Y 6JM/01-493 5021.
French Embassy (Cultural Department): 22 Wilton Crescentt, London SW1X 8SB/01-235 8080.

Andorra Representative: c/o Marie-Rose Picart de Francis, 63 Westover Road, London SW18 2RS/01-874 4806.
Boulogne Chamber of Commerce: Biss Lancaster, 2 Tavistock Place, London WC1H 9RA/01-278 4334.
Calais Chamber of Commerce: 19 Hampstead Lane, London N6 4BR/01-348 0503
Food & Wine From France: Nuffield House, 41-46 Piccadilly, London W1V 9AJ/01-439 8371 (Write or telephone for information — No personal callers).
French Chamber of Commerce: French Chamber of Commerce House, 54 Conduit Street, London W1R 9SD/01-439 1735
French Trades Exhibition: French Chamber of Commerce House, 54 Conduit Street, London W1R 9SD/01-439 3964.
Monaco Information Bureau: 34 Sackville Street, London W1X 1DB/01-437 3660
War Graves Commission: 2 Marlow Road, Maidenhead, Berks SL6 7DX/0628 34221.

Car Ferry Connections Between the UK and France (Belgium)

Brittany Ferries	Portsmouth-St. Malo	9 hrs.
Millbay Docks	Plymouth-Roscoff	6 hrs.
Plymouth PL1 3EF		
Tel. (0752) 213121		
or		
Norman House		
Albert Johnson Quay		
Portsmouth PO2 7AE		
Tel. (0705) 27701		
North Sea Ferries	Hull-Zeebrugge	15 hrs.
King George Dock	(Belgium)	
Hull HU9 5QA		
P&O Ferries	Southampton-Le Havre	7 hrs.
Arundel Towers	Dover-Boulogne	1 hr. 40 mins.
Portland Terrace		
Southampton SO9 4AE		
Tel. (0304) 203399 or (0304) 34141		

Sally - The Viking Line	Ramsgate-Dunkerque	2½ hrs.
Ramsgate Harbour		
Kent CT11 8RP		
Tel. (0843) 55522		
or London 01-409 2240		
Sealink	Dover/Folkestone-	1¾ hrs.
	-Boulogne	
Sealink Car Ferry Centre	-Calais	1½ hrs./
		1 hr. 50 mins.
PO Box 303	-Dunkerque	2 hrs. 20 mins.
55 Grosvenor Gardens	-Ostend	3½/4¼ hrs.
London SW1W 0AG	(Belgium)	
Tel. 01-834 2345	Newhaven-Dieppe	4 hrs.
	Weymouth-Cherbourg	3 hrs. 55 mins./
		4 hrs. 25 mins.
Townsend Thoresen	Dover-Calais	1¼ hrs.
1 Camden Crescent	Dover-Zeebrugge	4½ hrs.
	(Belgium)	
Dover, Kent CT16 1LD	Southampton-Cherbourg	5 hrs.
Tel. (0304) 203388	Southampton-Le Havre	6½ hrs. day/
and		7¼-8½ hrs. night
127 Regent Street	Portsmouth-Cherbourg	4¼ hrs. day/
London W1R 8LB		6½ hrs. night
Tel. 01-734 4431	Portsmouth-Le Havre	5½ hrs.
and 01-437 7800		
Hoverspeed	Dover-Boulogne	35 mins.
International Hoverport	Dover-Calais	35 mins.
Ramsgate, Kent CT125HS	Ramsgate-Calais	40 mins.
Tel. (0843) 555555		
or London 01-499 9481		